Also available at all good book stores

9781785316470

9781785313929

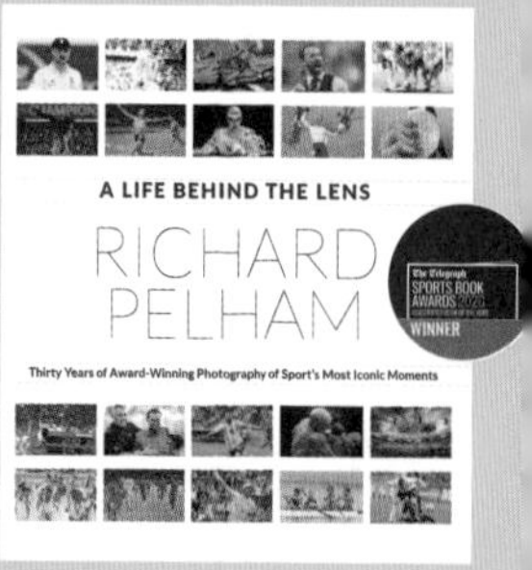

9781785315466

9781909178731

9781785318832

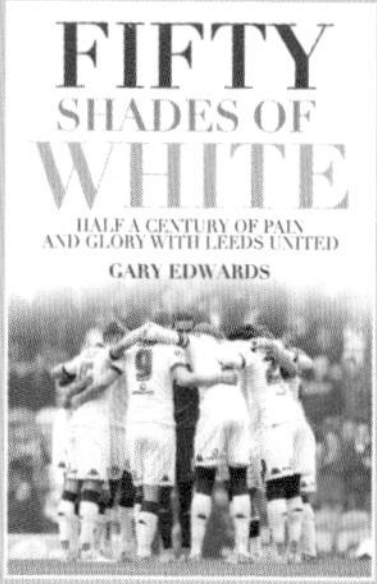

9781785311987

9781908051387

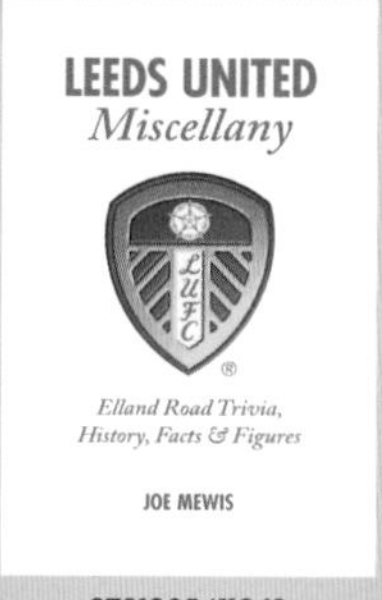

9781905411962

9781905411535

MARCELO
BIELSA
VS THE DAMNED UNITED

MARCELO BIELSA VS THE DAMNED UNITED

THE EXTRAORDINARY STORY OF
A CLUB REBORN

FOREWORD BY EDDIE GRAY

ROCCO DEAN

pitch

First published by Pitch Publishing, 2021

Pitch Publishing
A2 Yeoman Gate
Yeoman Way
Worthing
Sussex
BN13 3QZ
www.pitchpublishing.co.uk
info@pitchpublishing.co.uk

A CIP catalogue record is available for this book from the British Library.

ISBN 978 1 78531 993 8

Typesetting and origination by Pitch Publishing

Printed and bound in India by Replika Press Pvt. Ltd.

Contents

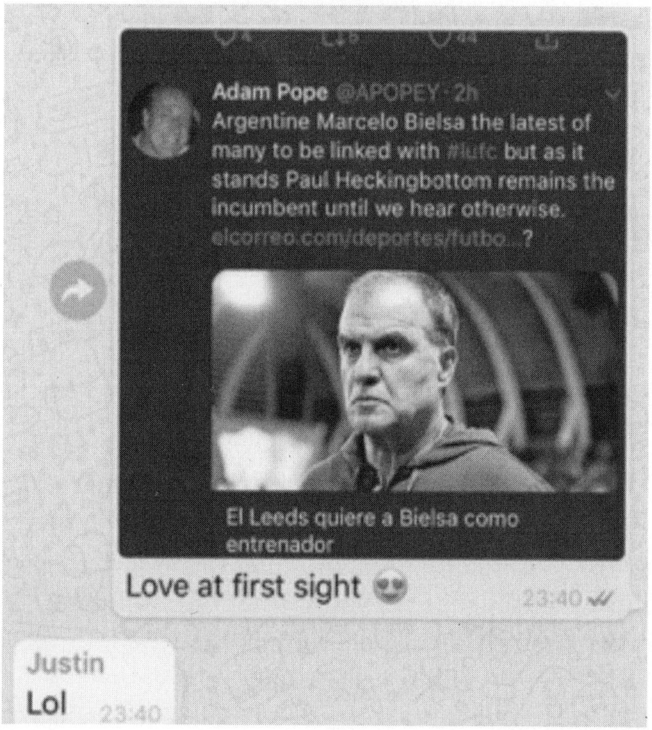
Adam Pope @APOPEY · 2h
Argentine Marcelo Bielsa the latest of many to be linked with #lufc but as it stands Paul Heckingbottom remains the incumbent until we hear otherwise.
elcorreo.com/deportes/futbo...?
El Leeds quiere a Bielsa como entrenador
Love at first sight
23:40
Justin
Lol
23:40

Dedication

Bielsa, his spontaneous visit to my house, and outlook on football and life, inspired me to turn a rambling account of an unforgettable season into the best work I could produce.

Italy's finest, Andrea Radrizzani, without whom this story would not exist.

Elland Road, a place I fell in love with the moment I stepped foot inside. I miss you every day!

Leeds fans; if they aren't the best in the world then they are certainly the best to be a part of.

Sandman, Alessandro Marcelo Dean, whose conception in early 2019 prompted me to document the Bielsa era.

And my wife, Frankie, for understanding.

Foreword by Eddie Gray

Marcelo Bielsa vs The Damned United is a fascinating read for fans of Leeds United. Written by a passionate supporter, it is a well researched match-by-match account of two memorable seasons as the club chased their goal of returning to the Premier League after a long and frustrating absence, led by a manager who transformed not just the team, but the city as a whole.

Having played for the club for almost 20 years and managed the club on two separate occasions, I have first-hand experience of the ups and downs Leeds United have experienced for over half a century, and there can be no doubt Elland Road had been a dark place when Marcelo Bielsa arrived. It was the home of a struggling Championship team, suffering the longest period outside the top flight in the club's history. The new manager brought fresh hope. This was an eccentric, enigmatic, and world-renowned coach, whose methods and philosophy had endeared him to supporters around the globe, and engrained him into the fabric of the places he had managed. Bielsa is idolised in Bilbao, Marseille, and Chile (where he managed the national team), while his first club, Newell's Old Boys, went as far as renaming their stadium Estadio Marcelo Bielsa.

The city of Leeds fell for him in the same way. Bielsa's morals and values resonated with the people of Yorkshire, and the feeling is mutual. It's a feeling I know well. I moved to the area from Glasgow as a 16-year-old boy, and over 50 years later it is the place my family calls home. Bielsa often speaks of feeling at home in Yorkshire, he is touched by the warmth and affection the people have shown him, and this feeling of belonging drove him to remain at the club in the aftermath of the heart-breaking play-off defeat to Derby County at the end of his first season. It was a near-miss that has been so common at Leeds United over the years, but with Bielsa committing to a second season in the English Championship the club was able to achieve their objective and finally return to the Premier League, albeit in unprecedented circumstances.

These two years under Marcelo Bielsa in many ways epitomised 100 years of Leeds United; it's never easy, there's always something or someone waiting to trip you up, and it's never over until it's over. The first season was one of the most eventful in the club's history; the second season provided redemption for the difficult times that the club had endured before Bielsa arrived. *Marcelo Bielsa vs The Damned United* captures all the emotions of a tumultuous journey, enabling Leeds fans to reminisce over an unforgettable period for years to come.

Eddie Gray

Introduction

IT WAS the first night of April 1994, Leeds United vs Newcastle United. I was ten years old, watching on Sky in my mum and dad's bed, adjudged too ill to attend. Andy Cole's 40th goal of the season separated the sides but Leeds had a 90th-minute corner, and as Gordon Strachan trotted over to the north-east corner flag, for the first time in my life I prayed for a goal. A higher power drew Pavel Srníček into no-man's-land, launched Chris Fairclough above Darren Peacock, and paralysed three Newcastle defenders on the goal line, who watched as the ball floated into the net. A point was ours, hallelujah! But Leeds were fifth in the Premier League and destined to finish there, not even high enough for European qualification in those days. What a waste of my one football miracle.

Through the next 16 years, every time I thought, 'I've never wanted to win more,' Leeds lost; 3-0 to Aston Villa in the League Cup Final, 1-0 to Wolves in the FA Cup quarter-final, 1-0 to Manchester United in the thick of a title race, 2-0 in the UEFA Cup semi-final, 3-0 to Valencia in the Champions League semi-final, 3-0 to Watford in the Championship play-off final, and 1-0 to Doncaster in the League One play-off final. If losing all seven games isn't depressing enough, consider that we didn't even manage to score a single goal, despite being the favourites in most of them. The barren run finally ended on 5 May 2010 with a 2-1 victory over Bristol Rovers to clinch second spot in League One, the glorious pinnacle of my lifetime supporting Leeds United. I console myself by thinking Bristol Rovers may well have been the most euphoric afternoon Elland Road has ever seen, although that in itself is pretty depressing too.

If I could take back my answered prayer and use it on another occasion, I'd choose Ipswich at home in 2007, when we were a minute away from relegation to the third tier of English football. Only a goal could save us, but when Trésor Kandol's flick-on ran harmlessly out of play for a goal kick, a minority of idiotic Leeds fans thought they could save us by invading the pitch. The players retreated to the tunnel and the rest of the crowd were incredulous, chanting, 'You're the scum, you're the scum, you're the scum of Elland Road!' To this day I've never been angrier; my bones were shaking, muscles pumping, baying for the mindless imbeciles to get off the fucking pitch. A bizarre scene turned unfathomable when the referee made an announcement through the PA system that if the pitch was cleared immediately they would play out the last minute, and the match would restart with a Leeds corner. It wasn't a corner in a million years, and we had been gifted a lifeline! So my muscles pumped harder, I screamed like my life depended on it, and the morons finally yielded. The players re-emerged and Alan Thompson trotted over to the north-east corner flag, which is when I should have prayed for a goal. I can barely imagine the scenes if we'd scored from that corner, but this is Leeds, The Damned United, and Thompson didn't even clear the first man.

Leeds's woes cannot be blamed on me, though. My answered prayer was just the Football Gods lulling a young boy into a false sense of security, the club was damned long before I was born. Our greatest manager, Don Revie, believed a gypsy curse had been placed upon Leeds United and tried to have it exorcised on two separate occasions between 1965 and 1973, when his team were runners-up five times in the league and four times in the cups, often in scandalous circumstances. Yet Don hadn't even seen the half of it (what a visionary).

Our greatest injustice came in the 1975 European Cup Final. Leeds battered defending champions Bayern Munich, but when Peter Lorimer lashed in what should have been the winning goal, Bayern captain Franz Beckenbauer convinced the referee to award offside, while the linesman stood upfield awaiting kick-off. This wasn't the only bizarre decision and Leeds eventually succumbed 2-0, though our fans claimed victory and still sing about our glorious triumph to this day. The aftermath was far from glorious and the Leeds fans rioted in the Parc des Princes and through the streets of Paris, resulting in a ban from European football and an abrupt end to the era.

Almost 50 years on and the Leeds supporters have never seen better days than that decade of desperate misfortune. Between 1975 and 2004 the club only won one major trophy, but that was nothing compared with the darkness to come; 14 years of lower-league football, terrible players, bewildering managers and despicable owners. The physical low was sitting 15 points adrift at the bottom of League One, but the peak of our torment was 2014/15, when Leeds were at their most shambolic under the ownership of Massimo Cellino. The season started with a winding-up order and a transfer embargo, by the end of October we were appointing our third 'permanent' manager, and by the end of the season Cellino was banned, the manager had no coaches or scouts, half a team refused to travel to a match at Charlton, and finishing 15th in the Championship was a huge relief.

I can't say I have no regrets, but the history of near-misses, failures, controversies and calamities forged a truly unique fanbase that is the allure of Leeds United. No similar-sized group in world football has experienced so little success, or suffered half as much pain. The desperation to right the wrongs of the past flows through our veins, culminating in a support that is fiercely passionate, ferociously partisan, and forever loyal.

Part One: 2018/19

THE SEASON THAT HAD EVERYTHING, EXCEPT A HAPPY ENDING

MARCELO BIELSA'S LEEDS UNITED

First of all there's the boss who's right behind us,
He's the one who fills our hearts with pride.
It's a joy to us all, when big Swede heads the ball,
To know that he is on our side.
There's a blonde-headed madman known as Gjanni,
And he goes like a human dynamo,
Patrick Bamford of course, he can work like a horse,
And top-knot Ayling's always on the go.

And we play all the way for Leeds United,
Elland Road is the only place for us,
With heart and soul for the goal that's clearly sighted,
We're out to toast each other from that silver cup.

Hear the roar when Kemar scores to lift the Roofe off,
Jackie Harrison's pillow feet are just sublime.
While the Pole is always there, doing more than his share,
Bera's side before self, every time.
Proud and tall at the coin-toss, Captain Cooper,
And the 11 Stus patrol down either wing,
Yorkshire Pirlo in pivot, then to tie 'em in a knot,
There's Pablo the Spanish King.

And we play all the way for Leeds United,
Elland Road is the only place for us,
With heart and soul for the goal that's clearly sighted,
We're out to toast each other from that silver cup.

Pre-Season 2018/19

MARCELO BIELSA came into my life at 11.35pm on 31 May 2018, when Justin posted on our LUFC WhatsApp group, 'Hope we get Bielsa.' I had no idea who he was, so turned to Wikipedia, as I did with all the new players and managers we were subjected to (the words paint a thousand pictures; you can't trust a YouTube highlights reel). At first glance Bielsa's record didn't look anything special. He'd won Argentinian titles, managed some big European clubs for short periods (including a worrying two-day stint with Lazio), and the national teams of Chile and Argentina with varying success. Despite the lack of trophies and longevity, it was obvious from his CV that he had something about him. I turned to Twitter to search for credible news and saw a photo of Bielsa, posted by Radio Leeds's Adam Pope, who was linking him with the job. I was immediately struck by Bielsa's intense glare; obsessive and serious, this guy would demand respect. At 11.40pm I responded to Justin with a screenshot of Popey's tweet, and captioned it, 'Love at first sight.'

The next morning, further research into Marcelo Bielsa turned my initial intrigue into desperation to appoint what was clearly a very special man. The so-called 'Godfather of Modern Football', Bielsa's methods and philosophy had spawned the new breed of managers at the very top of the world game today. Diego Simeone, Mauricio Pochettino and Zinedine Zidane were all 'disciples' of Bielsa, while Pep Guardiola, widely regarded as football's leading boss, had labelled Bielsa as 'the best coach in the world'. How could a club that had finished in the bottom half of the Championship in six of the past seven seasons attract a manager like this? And how had I never heard of him?

I also learnt about the origins of his nickname, 'El Loco' ('The Crazy One'), by reading about the time he confronted angry fans outside his home with a grenade in his hand, and watching grainy footage of a young Bielsa on the shoulders of those same fans, screaming amid wild celebrations, 'VAMOS NEWELLS CARAJO!' Later that day, manager Paul Heckingbottom was sacked. Now I was getting excited.

Current owner Andrea Radrizzani was a year into the job. He had increased the budget on the playing squad, professionalised the whole running of the club and, most significantly, bought back Elland Road. Putting our home back in the hands of the club was a tremendous statement, and helped keep the fans onside despite a miserable first season. The team went backwards after two cheap managerial appointments, while off the pitch there was the embarrassing release of a new badge 'for the next 100 years' that was so poorly received it was binned within six hours. The jury was still out on Radrizzani's ambition and judgement, but on the morning of 15 June it was announced that Marcelo Bielsa had agreed to become Leeds United manager and any questions about Radrizzani's ambition were put to bed. In terms of his judgement, well that would be defined by the results of 'The Bielsa Experiment', as it briefly became known.

In his first press conference you could tell Bielsa was a great man, yet doubts still lingered in my head. He confidently announced that we didn't need a new centre-back, that we had Pontus Jansson and Liam Cooper, and Gaetano Berardi and Kalvin Phillips could cover. This was absolutely baffling to me. I'd expected a new centre back to be the priority, a worthy partner for Jansson, the best defender in the league. Cooper had been at the club for four years without ever cementing his place in a predominantly useless team, and neither Berardi nor Phillips had ever played centre-back in their lives (neither would be considered tall enough). If Paul Heckingbottom had made such a suggestion then people may have burnt their season tickets before a ball was kicked, but there is a fine line between madness and genius and Bielsa had seen something in these players that we hadn't. He knew he could mould them into his system.

Doubts remained through pre-season; the friendlies didn't inspire confidence, nor did our transfer activity. There were only two permanent additions to the squad, and although Patrick Bamford was our most expensive signing in 17 years, every penny of the £7m fee was immediately recouped by selling prodigious midfielder Ronaldo Vieira to Sampdoria. Four loanees arrived from the Premier League, three of whom had underwhelmed in previous spells in the Championship, while the fourth was only halfway through a 12-month injury rehabilitation program.

However, the real work was going on behind the scenes. The players were training harder than ever; double sessions, triple sessions, daily weigh-ins, and the infamous 'Murderball' sessions (11 vs 11 played at maximum intensity, with no breaks in play). They were painstakingly drilled in the art of 'Bielsaball', and also trained in humility, made to spend three hours litter-picking around Boston Spa, the time it takes the average fan to earn enough money to watch them play.

By the eve of the new season the players couldn't wait to show everyone what they were capable of. Sky Sports was frothing at the mouth over Bielsa (or using him to sell more subscriptions), and I was flying back from a holiday in Sicily – not for the match, but for my wife's 30th birthday party.

August 2018

The Championship
First and second – promoted to Premier League
Third to sixth – play-off for last promotion spot
22nd to 24th – relegated to League One

Leeds United 3-1 Stoke City

A beautiful summer's day welcomed in the new season, but back in the old days, the grey and drizzly Paul Heckingbottom days, I had arranged to host a BBQ with our families for Frankie's birthday on Sunday, 5 August. I hadn't given the opening day of the season a second thought, but now the prospect of missing the grand opening of the Bielsa era was verging on catastrophic. After colluding with my dad on potential escape plans, common sense sadly prevailed and we would make do with watching it on telly.

The BBQ was a success, i.e. all the food was done by kick-off and we were able to watch the game from the sun-baked patio. 'We're going to get spanked,' declared Lewis while sharing the team sheet on WhatsApp. Reading through the same old names from last season, it was hard to disagree: Peacock-Farrell, Ayling, Berardi, Cooper, Douglas, Phillips, Klich, Hernández, Sáiz, Alioski, Roofe. Only one new addition to a team that finished last season at the bottom of the form guide, playing against relegated Stoke who had retained all their 'Premier League players', and added multimillion-pound signings to 'ensure' promotion.

But Leeds started brilliantly, playing at a fantastic tempo and even dominating possession. The players were visibly leaner, fitter and stronger; clearly they were following Bielsa's strict regime religiously. Thus it was no surprise when they took the lead after a lovely move cut through Stoke's defence and Mateusz Klich provided the cool finish. Klich had arrived at Leeds the previous summer but after just one start he was sent out on loan, back from whence he came, the Dutch Eredivisie. He wasn't even in Bielsa's plans initially, but after losing Adam Forshaw to injury and Ronaldo Vieira to Sampdoria, the door was left ajar and the popular Pole barged his way in, locked the door behind him, and threw away the key.

Significantly, Klich's goal did not change the game. Leeds continued to press like maniacs and the second goal followed when England's backup goalkeeper, Jack Butland, let a Hernández shot squirm through his hands and tickle the back of the net. At half-time we were in dreamland; 2-0 up and coasting against the favourites for promotion, the most expensive squad in the Championship.

In the second half I expected a backs-to-the-wall performance, and when Stoke pulled a goal back from the penalty spot I feared the worst. But Leeds responded in the best possible way, reinstating the two-goal advantage almost immediately, with Captain Cooper the deserving scorer. If I didn't already love El Loco, then his celebration of the third goal won my heart entirely. Sat on his bucket with hands clasped together, his body didn't move an inch but his fists shook ever so slightly when the ball hit the net. He just couldn't quite keep full control of his passion. Leeds saw out the victory in a professional and comfortable manner for an exceptionally impressive start to El Loco's reign.

After the game came the interview. Bielsa had never conducted a post-match interview as he only talks to the press at press conferences and hadn't spoken one-on-one to a journalist for decades. Contractually obliged, The Great Man insisted on conducting the interview in English, with the help of his translator, Salim Lamrani. To the naked eye, what followed was a hilarious spectacle showcasing Bielsa's 'loco' nature. Salim would translate the question to Bielsa, Bielsa would whisper his Spanish answer to Salim, Salim would whisper back the English translation of his answer, and Bielsa would repeat to the interviewer at least what he could remember of the English answer. You couldn't help but laugh, though while the public was laughing at Bielsa, I was laughing with him. This approach protected him from giving detailed answers before processing the match events, while showing a humble respect for the new country he was trying to adapt to. The genius had landed.

Derby County 1-4 Leeds United

After the fantastic performance against Stoke, the big question was whether Leeds could repeat it, and how often. There were also questions about the squad size, which was significantly smaller than the 25-man modern standard. In one of his famous long and captivating press conferences, Bielsa spoke of his preference for having 18 players of similar ability, with youth team players filling in when needed. This way, everyone would stay motivated and everyone would be an important part of the team. I liked the theory; pressing like maniacs over the marathon 46-game Championship season would be a big ask for such a small squad, but I was already starting to trust everything Bielsa said.

Leeds headed to Derby and I headed to the Straker wedding, sacrificing the chance to even watch on telly this time. Pride Park had not been a happy hunting ground for us in recent years as Leeds always seemed to be Derby's biggest game of the season and, more often than not, their players would respond. The rivalry between the clubs was born out of the bad relationship between their managers in the 1970s, and, while it wasn't quite Revie vs Clough, Sky did their best to hype up the clash of the new bosses, the master Marcelo Bielsa vs the apprentice Frank Lampard, who was one match into his managerial career. Lampard was very respectful in the build-up, supporting Sky's narrative by revealing that he had 'all Bielsa's books' on his shelves at home.

It was an evening kick-off, and as we sat down for the wedding breakfast I propped my phone against a spare glass and loaded Sky Go. Leeds were already 1-0 up! The lead didn't last long as, a few minutes later, Derby equalised from a free kick – a 'stunning strike' according to the commentators, though in reality it was a soft goal for young keeper Bailey Peacock-Farrell to concede. As they had against Stoke, Leeds responded brilliantly. Less than ten minutes later Alioski's pinpoint cross was met by an equally pinpoint header from Kemar Roofe, which looped gloriously into the far corner. I couldn't help letting out a 'GET IN!' in my now drunken excitement.

Being an upstanding citizen and respectful wedding guest, I turned off Sky Go for the speeches and just kept checking the score every few minutes; 2-1 became 3-1, and 3-1 became 4-1, I was absolutely blown away! In celebratory mood among a wedding full of Middlesbrough fans, I quickly went from absolutely hammered to waking up wondering if Leeds had really won at all. Twitter confirmed it wasn't a dream, and from all reports we were even more impressive against 'Frank Lampard's Derby County' than we had been against Stoke. Once home I was able to watch the footage for myself, and what a joy it was. With beautiful passing, relentless pressing, fantastic goals, it had been a true masterclass by the master, leaving Lampard scratching his head.

What a sensational start to the season; six points and seven goals when some people (me) may have accepted one point and one goal. I was now heading off to Canada for a work trip, but I would be back in the country just in time for the next game, to finally see Bielsa's Leeds in the flesh, to finally see Bielsa upon his bucket.

Leeds United 2-0 Rotherham United

By now, Bielsa-mania was in full swing, with press conferences dominated by questions about the 'bucket' Bielsa perched on in his technical area. It was all quite embarrassing, just serving to feed the El Loco caricature, yet The Great Man still answered the questions with his innate honesty: 'It is just a bucket, I cannot say any more than this. It is a comfortable bucket.' The bucket was added to the product line in the club shop, retailing at a whopping £80.

My pilgrimage to Elland Road began in Toronto on Friday evening. I had been miraculously allocated a seat in business class on the outward journey, and lightning struck twice on the flight back to Heathrow. 'Is your name Rocco?' asked the stewardess as I was boarding. It was my old school friend, Sarah, and a few minutes later I was being smuggled from my seat on the very back row into business class! I was cock-a-hoop, far too excited to make use of the flat beds and get even a wink of sleep.

I arrived home at noon, said hello to Frankie, showered, donned my new 'lucky' Bielsa top, and waved goodbye to Frankie, with my dad already waiting on the driveway, desperate for his fish and chips. Me and my dad have an arrangement where he pays for our season tickets and I buy the fish and chips. However, due to jet lag or a Freudian slip, today I hadn't brought any cash so Dad had to cough up. Just two home games in and he was effectively three fish and chips down on the deal. Once a season, fish and chips are not the pre-match highlight, eclipsed on the first home game by the sight of Elland Road as you walk down Beeston Hill. It's a glorious sight all year round, but especially so when basking in the August sun, and even more so after a 16-hour journey.

Over the summer, Andrea Radrizzani had been busy sprucing up the exterior of the stadium. The iconic statue of our greatest captain was now the centrepiece of 'Bremner Square', an area of personalised bricks bought and inscribed by fans. The south-east corner of the ground was already a focal point on matchday, but this new feature added nicely to the atmosphere among the scarf stalls, burger vans, and programme sellers on Lowfields Road. There was also an added buzz in the north-east corner of the ground, where the ticket office had been replaced by a fan park, transforming hordes of anxious queuers into tanked-up louts.

The final hurdle before entering the ground is always a nerve-wracking affair – the age-old battle of man vs machine. The automated turnstile has never malfunctioned, but one day it might, and this perpetual threat hangs over me every match until I am inside the Kop. My hatred for the automated turnstile isn't helped by the fact it cost me a job, for I was among the humble turnstile operators who were tragically made redundant in the summer of 2004. I lived the dream, being paid £25 a match to watch Leeds. My boss was a lovely bloke called Ray Gay who used to call me 'Deano', which I took as a sign of affection until receiving my first pay cheque, with 'Dino Rocko' written on the envelope. It's certainly not the first time my names have been mixed up (or misspelt), but I couldn't help chuckle at the irony of a man called Ray Gay mixing up my names.

After trudging through piss in order to take a piss in the Kop's unrefined toilets, I finally made it to my seat. It was a great feeling being back in the Kop, the only place for me. Within five minutes of kick-off I had texted the WhatsApp group, 'This is amazing.' It was so clear to see the difference; quick first-time passing, one-twos, rehearsed patterns of play. It was as if Bielsa had taught the players how to play football. Yet it was Rotherham who should have taken the lead when a misunderstanding while playing out from the back almost presented them with an open goal. Somehow Peacock-Farrell recovered to make the save and I couldn't help feeling it was a big moment in the season. Playing out from the back had cost Pep Guardiola's Manchester City many goals in his first season, so I assumed it would do so for Leeds. The key was avoiding any early-season calamities that would undermine the confidence of players and fans in the philosophy.

It was 0-0 at half-time but in the second half the pressure finally told and Leeds took the lead through Luke Ayling's first goal for the club, with the help of goal-line technology. I didn't even know we had goal-line technology, so it was very confusing when the goal was eventually awarded, but a huge relief. Now ahead, we began to flex our muscles. Some of our football was irresistible, and one move in particular was mindblowing, especially coming from the players of the previous season.

A long, calm build-up of passing across defence and midfield exploded into life with a series of one-twos that resulted with the ball at Sáiz's feet, and the goal at his mercy. The Spanish playmaker refused the chance to pass into the net – perhaps he thought the move had been too good for a simple finish – and instead he scooped the ball towards the top corner, where it was headed off the line. It would have been one of the best goals I've ever seen at Elland Road, more suited to

Barcelona than Beeston, but when the second goal did come we had to settle for one of the best in recent years. Under pressure deep in their own half, again Leeds would not simply clear the ball but played in triangles around the Rotherham attackers until Kalvin Phillips was free in midfield. The local boy lofted a magnificent 50-yard pass in behind the defence, Kemar Roofe beat the defender for pace, shrugged him off with his new-found strength, and from a tight angle (of which we had the perfect view) he lifted the ball into the far corner. Game, set, and match. Elland Road rejoiced.

As the players made their customary post-match lap of honour the Leeds fans lauded their new heroes, the same players who had been lambasted earlier in the summer. I knew they could fall back to their normal standard soon enough, but seeing that they were capable of playing such fantastic football was so exciting. I couldn't wait for the next match.

Swansea City 2-2 Leeds United

Leeds's tough start to the season continued with a long midweek trip to relegated Swansea. Unlike Stoke, Swansea had sold players, changed manager, and seemed fairly content with a re-building job in the Championship, but nevertheless this was still expected to be one of the most difficult away games of the season. The match was live on Sky, so I headed into town to watch it with my mates.

Complacency crept in during the pre-match merriment and by kick-off we were scampering around town, struggling to find somewhere to watch the game. We headed to Christies, an old favourite that held fond memories of rolling around the floor aged 21, celebrating a victory at Newcastle. To our horror Christies weren't showing the game, so we dashed up the hill to The Den, which held fond memories of rolling around the floor aged 33, celebrating a draw at Newcastle. The Den wasn't even open, so we dashed to the safe haven of The Alex, the main pub in Harrogate for watching live sport, which held my very fondest memory of watching football in a boozer. Not Newcastle-related this time, nor were we rolling around the floor, as it was completely covered in smashed glass from 300 or so dropped pints after Jonny Howson's last-gasp winner at Carlisle sent us to Wembley in 2008.

We arrived at The Alex 15 minutes into the game with the score still 0-0, but Swansea soon took the lead with a strike from outside the box that should never have beaten the keeper. I expected Leeds to cave in but again they responded well, equalising when youngster Jamie Shackleton burst to the byline and squared for Kemar Roofe to tap home. Roofe had arrived at the club two years earlier, a £3m marquee signing from League Two Oxford who couldn't nail down his best position, let alone a place in the team. Bielsa had made him an out-and-out striker; a good one, too, a livewire fox-in-the-box with four goals in four games this season.

In the second half Bielsa's side continued to play some good football, but it was no big surprise when Swansea's Leeds-born striker Oli McBurnie scored a fantastic looping header. Staring defeat in the face, Bielsa introduced this year's marquee signing, Patrick Bamford, and in the 79th minute a few slick passes sent Bamford racing down the left wing. Pat sent a harmless-looking low cross into the box, but it evaded the first defender and turned into a magnificent pass when Pablo Hernández popped up, nipping between two defenders to slot the ball calmly into the bottom corner of the net. It was another lovely goal, and another indication that the team's resolve had been significantly strengthened.

Swansea could have won it at the death, but Peacock-Farrell stood big and atoned for the soft goal he had conceded in the first half, securing a 2-2 draw, which felt like a point gained rather than two dropped. The feel-good factor continued unabated and we celebrated with too many Sambucas, too long into the night. By the morning there was no feel-good factor at my desk, or at the Thorpe Arch training ground, where the Leeds players received a two-hour hammering for all the things they had done wrong at Swansea. El Loco was setting the bar high; failing to win was not to be celebrated.

Norwich City 0-3 Leeds United

Saturday brought another long trip, to another ground where we always seem to struggle (I'm not sure there's a ground where we don't). There was no long trip for me though. Away days were sadly a thing of the past, and tickets are in such demand that if you don't go to every game you barely have a chance of going to any.

Instead I was hosting another birthday BBQ. It was a glorious summer's day, spent in the garden with Frankie and the full Purchase clan; my Manchester United-supporting mate, his wife, and all four godchildren. We fired up the BBQ, cracked open the beers and kicked a ball around while *Soccer Saturday* blared out of the kitchen. Despite Norwich's slow start to the season, and ever the pessimist, I assumed our bubble would burst today. Quite the opposite, the bubble soared! Within 20 minutes of kick-off, host Jeff Stelling announced, 'Goal at Carrow Road!' and I was surprised and delighted to hear that Mateusz Klich had put Leeds into the lead. Five minutes later, 'Another goal at Carrow Road … but which way has it gone?' To Leeds of course! Gjanni Alioski had doubled the lead. What a start, what a team!

We had to repel what sounded like a bit of an onslaught at the start of the second half, but Pablo Hernández soon delivered the knockout blow, curling in a peach of a goal from the corner of the box, sealing the three points and capping a superb individual performance. Hernández had been playing in Qatar when he joined Leeds in 2016 for next to nothing, and the similarities between him and the last man to lead the club out of this division (in the right direction), Gordon Strachan, were striking. They both came to Leeds in their 30s, the old men of the squad but still among the fittest players who dictate matches, scorers of important goals and special goals, model professionals and natural leaders, if only by example in Pablo's case.

In the post-match press-conference, Hernández received the highest praise from his manager. Bielsa is famed for improving players, and was asked whether he thought he could improve Pablo's game despite him entering the twilight years of his career. He replied, 'Hernández is so good he can improve me as a coach.'

Leeds United 0-0 Middlesbrough

It had been the hottest summer in my living memory, certainly since the hosepipe bans of the mid-1990s, and today was another scorcher. In anticipation of a mouth-watering Friday night top-of-the-table clash, I had booked the afternoon off work and headed to The Boathouse with Rick, our new favourite haunt for pre-game beers. It boasts a large beer garden that runs along the banks of the Leeds-Liverpool canal, perfect for a sunny day. As the afternoon progressed we were joined by the Woollards, then special guest Lewis, all the way from Canada. The special guest had his own special guest, Pontus Jansson's brother, who had befriended Lewis through post-match Twitter debriefs. Peter had travelled from Malmö for tonight's game and had arranged to come meet Lewis, but by the time he and his friends arrived I was 'a bit' drunk and didn't even introduce myself.

For most of my mates' football and drinking goes hand in hand, but they don't for me. I enjoy the drinking part, but the price you pay during the game just isn't worth it. I like to be fully engaged and fully wound up; boozing just dulls my senses (not to mention the dreaded double vision that can be induced). Thankfully, I managed to sober myself up by the time we got to the ground.

Sky billed tonight's game as Bielsaball vs Pulisball, a cheesy line but a valid reference to the clash of styles. Tony Pulis is the archetypal English manager (despite apparently being Welsh), and his direct and physical Middlesbrough team were strongly fancied to be one of the two winners of automatic promotion from the division. It promised to be the toughest test yet for Bielsaball in English football and proved to be just that. Boro had no problems with Bielsa's high press; their direct style simply bypassed it, thus Leeds struggled to dominate. A tense match unfolded, and despite a lack of goalmouth action it was a game I enjoyed; two top teams going toe-to-toe, a good, honest battle and a good advert for the Championship. Peacock-Farrell made a couple of big saves, there were a couple of big penalty shouts for each team, and in the end Middlesbrough were worthy of their point, and maybe more.

I left the ground feeling a little deflated and it was sobering (quite literally) to see Bielsa's Leeds team kept at bay. Nevertheless, it was a decent point on the board, and the clean sheet was a feather in the cap of El Loco, who had made a big pre-match call in bringing fit-again captain Liam Cooper back into the team, not in place of Berardi, as expected, but Sweden international Pontus Jansson. It was a major show of loyalty from The Great Man as Berardi had done everything asked of him and deserved to keep his place, even if it meant our best defender would watch the biggest match of the season so far from the bench. I'm not sure any other manager would have left out Jansson for this game as his aerial prowess alone was a big attribute to ignore against Pulisball, but it set down an early marker for the rest of the squad. Play well, and you will keep the shirt.

Leeds headed into the first international break as Championship leaders, but no one was getting carried away. We had been top at the same stage last season, playing stylish football under a foreign manager new to the English game, until a trip to The Den after the first international break derailed our season with a defeat the players later admitted they never recovered from. Waiting on the other side of this season's first international break was a trip to The Den.

September 2018

1	Leeds	14
2	Middlesbrough	14
3	Sheffield United	12
4	Derby County	12
5	Brentford	11
6	Bristol City	11

Millwall 1-1 Leeds United

In his first month in English football, El Loco was named manager of the month, but The Great Man refused to have his picture taken with the award. He didn't want to accept recognition when nothing had been achieved.

There was no such modesty from August's player of the month, Kemar Roofe, but his photo with the award was the last we'd see of him for a few weeks. Roofe had been struck down by injury, joining Pablo Hernández and Patrick Bamford in the treatment room; Pablo for a few weeks, Bamford a few months. Gaetano Berardi was also facing a period on the sidelines, but, as harsh as this is on Berardi, a lion-hearted defender who epitomises the club motto, 'Side Before Self', I was pleased that Pontus Jansson could now return to the team. Millwall would be another physical battle, the type Pontus relishes.

Another day, another wedding; the McTagues, on the bonny bonny banks of Loch Ken. This time it was a wedding full of Leeds fans, and the match fell kindly between the ceremony and breakfast, otherwise known as 'Mingling Hour'. I tried to stay relaxed by convincing myself that we never get anything at Millwall anyway, though deep down I was desperate for Bielsa not to fall foul in South Bermondsey.

Intermittent checks of the Sky Sports app told me Leeds were dominating, but the longer it stayed goalless the more I was expecting a Millwall goal to flash up. When Millwall did take the lead my lack of surprise didn't quell my disappointment. I was gutted, and struggling to hide it from anyone who tried to mingle with me. With the clock ticking down I was checking my phone frantically, then came the thrilling highlight of a beautiful day, 'GOAL: LEEDS. Harrison, 89'. A few minutes later and the match ended in a 1-1 draw. I was delighted; another point on the board, still unbeaten.

I watched the highlights the next day and revelled in the wonderful circumstances in which Leeds equalised. As injury time approached, Leeds won a throw-in and the ball trickled into the Millwall technical area. Their manager, Neil Harris, refused to return it and a melee ensued between players and staff; even Bielsa got involved. Leeds were finally able to take the throw-in and a few passes later Jack Harrison collected the ball on the edge of the box and planted it into the bottom corner. Have that! The thing that struck me most was the reaction of the players when the ball hit the net. Not one of them celebrated the goal, and their only focus was on was getting the ball back to the centre circle and winning the match. What a fantastic attitude El Loco had instilled.

After the game Bielsa apologised for his conduct in arguing with the Millwall bench, 'I have the obligation of not behaving like this; with more experience one should moderate his behaviour.' Harris initially swept the incident under the carpet, but by Monday morning he'd changed his tune, attacking Bielsa and labelling him 'a disgrace to English football'. It would prove to be a taste of things to come, English football's 'holier than thou' attitude would throw up one of the biggest stories of the season.

Leeds United 3-0 Preston North End

I was once again making the pilgrimage to Elland Road from abroad. I had been working in Amsterdam but was able to fly back just in time for the match, luckily for my dad, who could finally receive his first complimentary fish and chips of the season. Preston had already won at Elland Road this season – albeit in the League Cup, against a weakened team who clocked up over 20 shots and could have played all night without scoring – but they'd lost almost every other match and were rock bottom of the Championship. Nevertheless, Bielsa warned that they were a good team, sitting well below their real standing in the league.

Leeds started superbly, at the top of their passing game and in total control. My dad sensed a goal was coming and, seconds later, he was proved right when Liam Cooper's header somehow evaded the goalkeeper and defender on the line. While Leeds's champagne football was getting all the headlines, the transformation of Cooper was a major factor in the team's change in fortunes. Not only had he become rock-solid in defence, he was also Bielsa's first line of attack, initiating every move with a brave range of passing, zipping balls into midfield or spraying them 50 yards out to each wing. In a matter of weeks, Bielsa had turned 'League One Liam' into 'Super Duper Liam Cooper', one of the most improved players I'd ever seen, and a worthy captain of our great club.

In the second half Leeds turned the screw, and finally doubled the lead in the 74th minute when Phillips produced another beautiful ball over the top of the defence, this time for Tyler Roberts to chase. Tonight was Roberts's home debut, nine injury-ravaged months after signing from West Brom for over £2m. It was a big fee for a striker who had just turned 19, and after missing chances at Millwall you could forgive him for feeling under pressure to score his first Leeds goal. Plenty have buckled under less, but Roberts outpaced the defence and casually lobbed the keeper from 20 yards. Pace and grace – a deadly combination. At 2-0 the game was won but nobody inside Elland Road was content. Still the players hounded Preston, still the fans urged them on gleefully, still Bielsa's staff marched around the technical area bellowing instructions, and as the rain poured down in the final minutes, Roberts clinically headed home his second of the game, turning a great night into his night.

There could no longer be any doubt; Leeds were the real deal, and no amount of rain could dampen our spirits walking back up Beeston Hill. What Bielsa had done to this team was astonishing, but what I found most fascinating was how he knew it would be possible based on footage from last season's shoddy performances (El Loco had watched all 51 of our matches in preparation for his first meeting with the club). A true football genius.

Leeds United 1-2 Birmingham City

Garry Monk did a great job as manager of Leeds in the 2016/17 season, turning a team with no heart and no hope into quite the opposite. Unfortunately, the unlikely promotion push tailed off in April, and two months later Monk was at Middlesbrough and Leeds were back to square one. I'm still not sure we know the full story, but Monk is always guaranteed a hot reception when returning to Elland Road, and today he returned with a Birmingham team he'd steered to safety on the final day of the previous season. Despite many good performances Birmingham were yet to register a victory this season, but again Bielsa urged caution as, like Preston, he believed they were a team sitting well below their true level.

The match quickly settled into what was now the standard rhythm. Leeds would control from the back, using the goalkeeper to work their way out of any high press and set up camp in opposition territory. But after ten minutes Elland Road was stunned into silence as a speculative shot by Che Adams somehow wrong-footed Peacock-Farrell and bobbled into the centre of the goal. By the half-hour mark it was 2-0, from another weak Adams shot that at least found the corner this time, but again my finger of blame pointed squarely at Northern Ireland's new number one.

With their unbeaten record on the line, Leeds attempted a second-half onslaught, though momentum was constantly tempered by outrageous time-wasting, with goal kicks developing into a pantomime that had the Kop seething. The non-stop bundle of energy, Gjanni Alioski, would sprint to retrieve every dead ball and place it in the corner of the six-yard box to save time, but every time the keeper would move it to the middle of the box, as slowly as he could. Like a lab rat, Alioski eventually learned, but when he finally placed the ball in the centre the keeper suddenly changed his preference and started taking his kicks from the corner again!

Birmingham invented another time-wasting tactic I'd never seen before, picking fights with Leeds players to create 22-man melees as the clock ticked down. By the time 90 minutes were up, chief ball boy Alioski had halved the deficit, and the fourth official indicated there would be a minimum of eight minutes of added time. Elland Road roared its approval. When chasing a game in injury time all you hope for is one chance, and it usually does come in some form. Today it came when Stuart Dallas made himself some space on the edge of the box, but his clean strike was superbly tipped around the post. Birmingham's winless run was over, and Leeds's unbeaten run had come to an end.

It was our first taste of a defeated El Loco, and while us mere mortals blamed the defeat on the referee, the time-wasting, our goalkeeper, and the predictably unpredictable nature of the Championship, The Great Man blamed himself. He normally plays his famous 3-3-1-3 formation when facing two strikers, but on this occasion he'd decided to stick to what was working. Kalvin Phillips was substituted after half an hour in order to make the tactical correction, but in the eyes of Bielsa it was too late; his mistake had cost Leeds three points. Taking the blame was not an attempt to take pressure off the players or to appear humble. Bielsa explains and justifies what he says with genuine reasoning, not hot air and clichés like his peers. In defeat, I was even more grateful to have him at the helm.

Sheffield Wednesday 1-1 Leeds United

As a member of the 'Against Modern Football' brigade (which refers to the changes off the pitch and mustn't be confused with Bielsa's revolutionary tactics) I should be firmly against football on a Friday night, but I have to admit I love it. For starters it makes the working week a day shorter; Thursday turns into Friday, and Friday turns into a total waste of time as you are too excited for the match. With a good result you can bask in the glory all weekend as your rivals toil, and with a bad result you have more recovery time. Rarely will it ruin the whole weekend.

It was six years since we last played at Hillsborough on a Friday night. I wasn't there that night, but watching on telly you could sense the atmosphere in the Leeds end was supercharged. Leeds equalised in the second half, sending the fans behind the goal delirious, one of whom ran on to the pitch and violently shoved Wednesday keeper Chris Kirkland in the face; a barbaric act on a player who had no previous history with Leeds. Sheffield Wednesday manager Dave Jones' post-match assessment was alarmingly blunt, 'Vile animals. All of them.' Wow, thanks Dave!

You would think they'd never put this fixture on a Friday night again, but here we were. I went to my sister's to watch it with my nephew, Lucca. We both expected a really tough Yorkshire derby and were taken aback by the extent of our dominance. It was wave after wave of Leeds attacks, but chance after chance went begging. In true Bielsa style, it was the full-backs who were most guilty in front of goal, and in true Leeds style, there was one hell of a sucker-punch, Wednesday's Adam Reach looping a stunning 40-yard volley high over Peacock-Farrell and down into the net via the post. It was one of those goals that leaves you wondering why some random always turns into van Basten/Gerrard/Messi against Leeds, although in this instance the lad had actually done it before, a couple of times, and would do it again only a few weeks later.

In the second half Leeds pushed harder and harder, and just when it was starting to look like Wednesday would never buckle, a lovely piece of play ended with a 30-yard curler from Klich into the top corner. It was such a wonderfully executed finish that you could legitimately question whether Reach's goal-of-the-season contender was even the goal of the game. Klich had been a revelation under Bielsa; tall and imposing, fit as a fiddle, classy with the ball at his feet, aggressive in winning it back, and an eye for goal. Exactly the type of midfielder we could have done with last season.

The game ended in a draw, a result I would have taken beforehand but certainly not by the end. The story of the match was reflected by the scene at the final whistle; the Leeds players stood watching the highlights on the big screen, wondering how on earth they had managed to come away with only one point. Nevertheless, the calibre of the performance overshadowed any disappointment, and despite the victories drying up I was even more confident that we were in for a great season. In his post-match interview (now conducted in the normal translated fashion), Bielsa bemoaned the missed chances, 25 by his count, but also revealed his jovial side for the first time when the interviewer referenced the 'many trophies' he had won in his career. Without hesitation, El Loco called him out, calling himself out in the process: 'It would not be difficult to find out that I have not won much in my career at all.'

Leeds had very quickly quashed my fears that they couldn't repeat the levels of the Stoke game, and were well on the way to quashing my fears that they couldn't play with such intensity in the long run. My remaining fear was how they would respond when results started to go against them, and whether the players would remain true to Bielsa's philosophy and hugely demanding lifestyle. With one win in four games, perhaps we would find out as autumn turned to winter.

October 2018

1	West Brom	20
2	**Leeds**	**19**
3	Middlesbrough	19
4	Sheffield United	19
5	Norwich City	17
6	Brentford	16

Hull City 0-1 Leeds United

Another Yorkshire derby away from home and under the lights, and this time I watched at my dad's courtesy of Sky's new Red Button service, through which all midweek Championship fixtures were available to view live. There was only one camera and no replays, but that mattered not; it was a huge bonus for those fans who can't commit to away games.

Despite Hull's struggles at the bottom of the table, I expected a tough battle from Nigel Adkins's men and was left shocked at how poor and unambitious they were. The hosts seemed to have no interest in venturing out of their own half or winning the ball back. It was as if they were just waiting for Leeds to score.

The wait lasted until early in the second half and it was another lovely goal to add to an ever-growing collection, Tyler Roberts fizzing a rocket of a shot into the bottom corner after some lovely build-up play. The joy at the beauty of the goal and the relief of a broken deadlock were in equal measure.

Frustratingly, Leeds failed to press home their advantage, and in the closing stages Hull finally came out of their shell. My agitation grew as the Leeds defence dropped deeper and deeper, and eventually they were officially hanging on. I always used to find it funny when my boss, Chris, would complain about his beloved Spurs team *only* winning 1-0, but I found myself with the same feeling; it was sloppy and careless that our nerves were being jangled so violently. Hull piled on the pressure, but some heroic injury-time defending from Jansson and Cooper preserved the advantage and Leeds were back to winning ways.

While delighted with the three points, this was the first time I hadn't enjoyed a Leeds game under Bielsa. Was I becoming spoilt by the brilliant football, or was I just becoming nervous about the opportunity that lay in front of us? Probably both, and this miserable anxiety would repeat itself time and time again as the season progressed.

Leeds United 1-1 Brentford

It was back to Elland Road for a televised lunchtime kick-off against high-flying Brentford, whose transfer policy of buying low and selling high was paying dividends. In the summer they had sold £20m of players but still had serious quality in attack, with Sergi Canós, Saïd Benrahma and Ollie Watkins supporting goal machine Neal Maupay. Dean Smith's men were shaping up to be a genuine rival for automatic promotion so this was going to be a tough afternoon for Leeds.

It really was a tough afternoon. Brentford's passing game was better than Leeds's and they kept Bielsa's team on the back foot throughout the first half. Thankfully the defence would not be breached, so the most noteworthy incident of the half came in the stands and my first encounter with the bloke in front of me. After I expressed my dissatisfaction following a Stuart Dallas mistake he asked, 'Do you not like Dallas?' 'I like him, I just don't think he's good enough,' which was a much less partisan statement compared to my previous outburst. The reply followed, 'Oh right, cos he thinks you're a c***!' I could only laugh, taking the comment in good spirits, although the delivery was so dry it did make me wonder for a few home games.

The second half was following a similar path to the first until the referee lit the blue touchpaper on the hour, exploding the game into life. Watkins was sent through on goal and clipped the ball over Peacock-Farrell, but thankfully Luke Ayling was covering and hoofed clear before it crossed the line. However, after applying his finish Watkins had flung himself to the floor, a good yard before he reached the onrushing keeper, and the referee inexplicably awarded a penalty. Maupay converted the penalty and goaded the South Stand, who duly showered him with a flurry of 'missiles'.

Leeds were really fired up now, with the players going hell for leather for an equaliser and the fans doing their best to suck the ball into the net. In the 88th minute Brentford finally wilted when a deep free kick was powered home by the head of Pontus Jansson. It was no more than Pontus deserved, having been in 'beast mode' all game. The players celebrated right in front of us and plenty of fans couldn't contain their excitement and spilled on to the pitch.

Leeds almost stole all three points in injury time through Chelsea loanee Lewis Baker, but his clever backheel (the only decent thing he did in a Leeds shirt) drifted inches wide. In the end everyone was happy enough with a point. Well, nearly everyone. In an onfield interview straight after the match, the interviewer asked Jansson how he was feeling, presumably expecting the imminent new dad, match saviour and man of the match to be on top of the world. 'Shit. I feel shit. I won't apologise, that was a robbery from the referee.' Never change, Pontus!

Despite dropping more points and slipping out of the automatic promotion spots, I left the ground exhilarated. I felt proud to the point of smugness that Elland Road was such a vibrant place to watch football, especially compared to Premier League grounds stifled by commercialism and day-trippers. The drama of the game didn't half help either. Where else other than at a football ground can you experience outrage, anxiety, hope, delight, relief and pride, all within half an hour? And be called a c*** along the way!

Blackburn Rovers 2-1 Leeds United

Another televised Saturday lunchtime kick-off brought another race against time to make it home for the game. I was again travelling back from Canada, though this time I was forced to slum it with the peasants in economy. I made it home just in the nick of time, tired but buoyed by the team news; Kemar Roofe was back in the team, and Pablo Hernández was back on the bench. Blackburn had a terrific recent home record, but with 8,000 Leeds fans packing out the Darwen End, today would feel more like an away game for them.

Blackburn silenced the away fans after just two minutes, taking the lead from a from a terribly defended corner. After 25 years supporting Leeds it would take more than a few months of good football to recalibrate my brain, but I was aware that my reflex reaction of 'here we go again' was grossly unfair. This was Bielsa's Leeds, and there were 88 minutes to turn the game around.

For the rest of the half Leeds controlled possession without troubling the deep-lying Blackburn defence, but when the clock struck 45 minutes one of my favourite goals of the season followed. Leeds had a throw-in in their own half and over the tannoy it was announced there would be one minute of added time. The players knew they only had a minute to score, but there was no panic as they shifted the ball patiently from left to right, waiting for an opening in midfield. That opening came with 15 seconds left on the clock. Sáiz seized the space and played a lovely ball over to Berardi, who squared it for Klich to tap in to the net with the last kick of the half. What a beautiful team goal – an exhibition of the skills they had learnt from Bielsa, and their unwavering belief in his philosophy.

By the time the second half kicked off I had been up for 36 hours, yet there was no chance of me dozing off as Leeds searched for the winning goal. But on 70 minutes disaster struck with another Blackburn corner and another soft Blackburn goal.

Leeds pressed for an equaliser but as time passed it looked less and less likely to come, and with his final throw of the dice Bielsa turned to Jack Clarke, a 17-year-old who was on fire for the under-23s. Immediately you could see the lad was a real talent as he almost created three goals for himself and looked like he could go his whole career without getting tackled, but ultimately there was no equaliser and Leeds dropped down to fourth place.

The form was becoming a bit of a problem, with only two wins in eight matches, but even so, my optimism remained high. Leeds were still playing well and had totally dominated a good side on their own patch again. Leeds were stronger, fitter, and simply a class above Blackburn, but mistakes at both ends of the pitch are a great leveller. Failing to take chances, or 'efficiency' as Bielsa called it, would get a lot of airtime in the coming months.

Leeds United 2-0 Ipswich Town

A midweek game against bottom-of-the-league Ipswich presented Leeds with the perfect opportunity to bounce straight back, although they were dealt a blow on the eve of the game, with Pontus Jansson receiving a one-match ban for his 'foul and abusive language' after the Brentford match. You couldn't dispute the punishment, but 17 days had passed since the incident and an earlier ruling would have given Pontus more time with his new-born daughter back home in Sweden. I couldn't help feeling there was some malice in the timing. Furthermore, there was no action taken for the clear dive that won Brentford a penalty and, more incredibly, Sergi Canós was cleared of any wrongdoing despite clearly being caught on camera head-butting Gjanni Alioski. Would the EFL ever change?

With Pontus suspended, Kalvin Phillips stepped in at centre-back for the first time. Phillips had been majestic in defensive midfield, so good that he had been dubbed 'The Yorkshire Pirlo'. Tonight he was even better at centre-back. Quick to the ball, strong in the tackle, so composed in possession, The Yorkshire Pirlo had morphed into Fabio Cannavaro. I've always loved Phillips – a Leeds lad, always with a big smile on his face, loving a tackle, and loving playing for Leeds – but he had endured a difficult start to his career and there would have been little outrage had Bielsa discarded him for a few hundred grand. Instead, Bielsa had turned him into one of the best players in the league.

Leeds dominated from start to finish. Hernández was back from injury and ran Phillips close for the man of the match award, and together they controlled the game; Phillips central to all the build-up play, Pablo turning the possession into chances. One of the first chances Pablo created was headed home by Kemar Roofe, who had returned without a bang against Blackburn but was back in the swing of things now. It was great to see the returnees combining for the opening goal.

Adam Forshaw was also back from injury, and his introduction in the second half added even more authority to the midfield, meaning Ipswich really had no chance. The second goal came from a quick short-corner routine that caught them cold. Pablo was the architect when his cutback, via a clever dummy, was drilled into the top corner by Liam Cooper. It looked like a training-ground move but it must have been organic; they surely couldn't have concocted a routine based around Liam Cooper smashing it into 'top bins' with his weaker right foot? Well, they do call Bielsa 'El Loco'.

This was a win that would gain no plaudits, but every match in the Championship is a potential banana skin and Leeds had dispatched their opponents in style. As the players took their lap of honour, the other results flashed up on the big screen to gleeful cheers; the rivals had dropped points and Bielsa's boys were back on top of the league.

Leeds United 1-1 Nottingham Forest

Saturday evening brought a hotly anticipated clash. Forest had made a good start under Aitor Karanka and this would be another stern test for Leeds. My dad was on holiday so I drove alone, listening to BBC Radio 5 Live as the final scores from the afternoon fixtures pushed Leeds back out of the top two. I swapped fish and chips for a rare pre-match pint in the Kop, where there was a real air of excitement despite mixed feelings regarding the team news. Pontus Jansson was reinstated after his suspension, but the mercurial Samu Sáiz had been dropped to the bench. Last season Sáiz burst on to the scene with a series of mesmeric displays, before a lengthy ban for spitting derailed his season. For all his silky play this season, his output in the final third had been frustratingly poor, but even so it was a big surprise to see him benched for such a big home game.

Adam Forshaw, the man Bielsa labelled as Leeds's best player when he arrived, took Sáiz's place in the team and grabbed his opportunity with both hands. It was probably Forshaw's best game in a Leeds shirt. His aggressive play set the tone and he almost opened the scoring with a scorching drive that sailed inches wide. But against the run of play it was Forest who held the half-time lead – another corner, another sloppy goal. Leeds were up against it again.

After the break it was men against boys and Forest couldn't get out of their own half as the home backline mopped up anything that managed to get past the rampaging midfield trio of Phillips, Klich, and Forshaw. The Leeds fans were stepping up to the plate too. One of the great sights of English football must be Elland Road singing, 'We are champions, champions of Europe' at full throttle, and it bellowed around the ground accompanied by thousands of swinging scarves and wave after wave of attacks. This was the Leeds United I fell in love with.

The mighty whites pushed and pushed but Forest wouldn't buckle, nor would the referee, who was so intent on not being swayed by the Elland Road crowd that he overcompensated in the away team's favour time and again. I had remained philosophical over the fact that Leeds had gone over a year without being awarded a penalty, but I lost the plot when Roofe was upended in the box, only for the visitors to be awarded a free kick.

Forest and the referee finally buckled in the 82nd minute when Leeds equalised in controversial circumstances. For once the incompetence of the officials went in Leeds's favour as they failed to notice that Roofe had diverted Klich's drive into the net with his hand, but the wild celebrations were put on hold as a swarm of red shirts marched the referee over to consult with his linesman, my heart was in my mouth. Taking advantage of my aisle seat, I rushed down to the front of the upper section of the Kop, leaned over the railings and screamed at the bastard ref not to disallow the goal. I was beside myself! I may have burst if the outcome had been different, but his arm eventually swung towards the centre circle and the wild celebrations resumed. There was no winning goal to send Leeds back to the top of the league but the draw was enough to shunt them back into the automatic promotion spots; a welcome second prize.

As there had been after the Blackburn game, there were complaints, that Leeds should be scoring more goals and making more clear-cut chances from all their possession, but anyone who was at Elland Road – or anyone with a memory longer than six months – must have loved this match. The team did us so proud; battling and fighting for every ball, players feeding off the fans and fans feeding off the players, a world away from what we'd become used to over the past decade. You have to be grateful for times like these, win, lose, or draw.

November 2018

1	Sheffield United	29
2	**Leeds**	**27**
3	Middlesbrough	27
4	Norwich City	27
5	West Brom	25
6	Derby County	25

Wigan Athletic 1-2 Leeds United

Today marked Dave Whelan's emotional farewell as owner of Wigan after an incredibly successful 20 years. I was concerned the Football Gods would help Wigan send the town's favourite son off in style, but instead the game would be remembered for ten seconds that showcased the incredible desire of Marcelo Bielsa's Leeds team.

It was another televised game, this time the Sunday lunchtime slot, so I settled down in the lounge while Frankie cooked me a roast dinner. Not too shabby. Luke Ayling was the latest victim of the incessant spate of injuries, ruled out for a couple of months after hobbling off against Forest. Known as 'Bill' to his team-mates (and manager, to my amusement), Ayling was a top Championship right-back even before El Loco got his hands on him, and one of only five 'specialist' defenders in the squad. This was a major blow that fuelled debate over whether Bielsa's training and tactics were too intense. We were only three months into the season and seven first-team regulars had already suffered significant injuries, yet Bielsa wouldn't be drawn on the subject. Injuries were normal; his job was to find the solutions.

It was no surprise that Leeds stamped their authority on the match right from the start, and when Wigan got a free kick on the edge of the box it was no surprise that Reece James morphed into Steven Gerrard and thundered it into the net. Leeds had fallen into a terrible habit of conceding the first goal, but they also had a good habit of rallying, and it wasn't long before some neat play split the Wigan defence for Pablo to tap in the equaliser. My half-time ablutions took longer than anticipated, and on my return to the lounge the Leeds players were already celebrating – what a lovely surprise! The goal came from a farcical mix-up between defender and goalkeeper, allowing Roofe to nick the ball from between them and roll it into the empty net.

Then came the highlight of the match. A Leeds corner was cleared up to Josh Windass, who set off on a run to goal with only Liam Cooper in his way. A few seconds later he was surrounded by a sea of white shirts, no less than seven, who won the ball back and started up the next attack. It was a glorious sight to behold and nothing I've ever seen the like of on a professional football pitch; everyone busting a gut, none of the seven content to leave his mates to it, even with no other Wigan player in support. What a will to win!

Young Jamie Shackleton's first professional goal would have sealed a comfortable victory, but his shot was blocked on the line by Roofe, so I was again left frustrated that we had to endure another nervy finish (spoilt brat). Wigan's push for an equaliser consisted of a flurry of long throws, but Pontus and Cooper eat long throws for Sunday lunch and Leeds returned to the top of the league. Frankie's roast has never tasted so good.

West Bromwich Albion 4-1 Leeds United

For the sixth weekend running we were denied a traditional Saturday 3pm kick-off, yet Sky's insatiable appetite for Leeds was not due to the Bielsa effect, the outstanding football, nor the promotion race. No matter how useless, Leeds have always remained the most televised team in the league; the biggest club guaranteeing the largest viewing figures. It was a bone of contention for owner Andrea Radrizzani (and previous owners too) that Leeds would be televised as much as the top clubs in the country, pulling in similar viewing figures but earning a tiny fraction of the TV revenue. This scenario highlights the gulf between England's top two divisions, and explains why the Championship is one of the biggest leagues in the world; it has the most lucrative prize.

As expected, West Brom were among the early-season pacesetters, and were also the division's top scorers. Dwight Gayle, Jay Rodriguez, and Harvey Barnes formed a formidable three-pronged attack, with former England internationals Gareth Barry and Jake Livermore holding in midfield and former Leeds captain Kyle Bartley struggling to get a game in defence. This would be the toughest test of the season so far.

It was my 35th birthday and Frankie had booked a night away, so I watched the match on Sky Go while Frankie spruced herself up for dinner. It was even in the first half, with West Brom coming closest to scoring when they rattled the Leeds crossbar, while at the other end wastefulness in the final third scuppered many visiting attacks. Early in the second half more wastefulness led to the opening goal. Mateusz Klich found himself alone in the middle of the box, eight yards out with the goal at his mercy, but for some reason he elected not to shoot and tried to tee up Harrison instead. Moments later the chance had gone, and moments after that the ball was in the Leeds net. The next 30 minutes were horrible as Leeds had all the play but couldn't score, and conceded goal after goal at the other end. Happy Birthday!

At 4-0 I decided enough was enough and went downstairs to drown my sorrows. To my credit I managed to get over the result quite quickly, filing it in the 'one of those days' category. There really was no need to panic as West Brom were a top side and on another day Leeds would have scored first and probably beaten them. At peace with the result (4-1 in the end) I did have a happy birthday. I've had worse after all; I spent my 30th watching a Leeds team managed by Neil Warnock lose 6-1 at home to Watford!

Leeds United 2-0 Bristol City

The two-week international break gave Bielsa and his team a lot of thinking time, and the fans a lot of overthinking time. Leeds had won only four of their last 13 games since sweeping aside Norwich, a team who had now charged ahead and were setting the pace at the top. Results may have given the impression that the players were returning to their old ways, but only the Twitterati really believed that.

During the break the injury curse hit again, striking down goalkeeper Jamal Blackman for the rest of the season, thus bringing a premature end to his loan from Chelsea. El Loco praised Blackman in his pre-match presser, surprising everyone when admitting that Blackman would have started this game ahead of Peacock-Farrell. Bielsa wanted the world to know that Blackman had reached the level required to become a starter. I loved the manager's honesty – so refreshing in a football world where sincerity has been replaced with buzzwords, clichés, and answers that don't actually answer anything – but I had to question whether it was wise. The praise for Chelsea's reserve keeper may have been deserved, but was it really worth the potential damage to our own youngster's fragile confidence? My doubts would be put in their place within days.

As it happened, Peacock-Farrell didn't play anyway as the injury curse accounted for him too, and Pontus Jansson, but at least these were expected to be short-term absences. Bielsa shunned the option of signing an emergency loanee, preferring to give the chance to our youth team goalkeeper, Will Huffer. The Great Man would never shirk at throwing in the academy lads and Huffer wasn't the only debutant, with big Finn Aapo Halme deputising for the big Swede. After a couple of early hiccups both youngsters performed well under little pressure as Leeds controlled the game from start to finish.

Nobody managed to score in the first half, but I told my mates at home not to worry; the Kop would suck the ball into the net after the restart. Our job was made easier when the visitors were reduced to ten men early in the second half, and having been patiently camped in opposition territory, Leeds now laid siege to the goal. With the game entering its final quarter the Kop finally sucked the ball in, via the foot of fox-in-the-box Kemar Roofe. Soon after that we were treated to a second goal and a nice calm finish to the game, thanks to a lovely looping Hernández header.

Bielsa was delighted with the performance, and was bemused at Bristol City manager Lee Johnson's claims that Leeds were lucky: 'We have to take into account the opinions of our rival when analysing this game, but I cannot agree that we did not deserve to win. We created many dangerous actions, while not conceding any chances ourselves.'

It had been the perfect response to the West Brom defeat, but bouncing back from disappointing results will only get you so far. What Leeds really craved was consistency, as they hadn't had successive wins since the opening weeks of the season. They were about to get lots of them.

Leeds United 1-0 Reading

I was on my travels again, this time in Scandinavia, so was forced to miss another home game, while my dad was again forced to pay for his own fish and chips. I'd accidentally booked myself a hellhole of a hotel on the outskirts of Copenhagen, but my disappointment was outweighed by the joy of discovering I was able to watch live on Sky Go (maybe Sky TV aren't so bad after all). Before the game Bielsa elaborated on his pre-Bristol comments regarding Bailey Peacock-Farrell: 'It was important for Farrell to know that he was going to be dropped; only through these setbacks can you improve as a player.' The young goalkeeper had recovered from injury and was back in goal, and tonight we would find out in the most dramatic of fashions the effect of Bielsa's man-management.

Reading were languishing at the bottom end of the table and Leeds came racing out of the blocks. A great chance went begging inside 30 seconds, but as the half wore on we became less and less dangerous. It was becoming quite a familiar theme; Leeds in total control but lacking a cutting edge. At half-time I called for the introduction of Sáiz and Clarke, and The Great Man duly delivered. It probably wasn't rocket science, but I couldn't help getting a buzz from El Loco seeing things the same as me. Leeds upped the intensity and as the game approached the latter stages their full-backs combined to break the deadlock, Stuart Dallas smashing a loose ball into the net from seven yards after good work by Douglas. Leeds were closing in on those elusive successive victories.

Reading had barely threatened all game, but with 90 minutes up there was still time for two twists to the plot. A rare foray into the Leeds box enticed Barry Douglas into a mindless lunge that gave away a stonewall penalty and surely two points with it. The scene was set for Peacock-Farrell to make himself a hero – and he did just that. Diving low to his right, the Peacock brilliantly turned a decent penalty around the post to win Leeds the match. Well done young man! The celebrations were as wild on the pitch as they looked in the stands, while the other guests in the Zleep Hotel wondered whether a crazed murderer was on the loose.

It felt like a big moment in the season. An amazing turn of events secured two extra points, pushed Leeds back into the top two and turned a mundane victory into a stunning victory. The Parable of the Dropped Goalkeeper; more proof that El Loco is a genius of his trade.

December 2018

1	Norwich City	37
2	**Leeds**	**36**
3	Middlesbrough	35
4	West Brom	34
5	Sheffield United	34
6	Nottingham Forest	31

Sheffield United 0-1 Leeds United

Saturday lunchtime brought a big Yorkshire derby, with Sheffield United on Leeds's heels and looking a better side than the one that fell away in the final stages of last season. Billy Sharp was scoring goals, their defence was one of the best in the league, and Marcelo Bielsa had plenty of pre-match praise for their unique style of play (3-5-2 with overlapping centre-backs): 'The ideas of our next opponent deserve to be studied. I see things in Sheffield United that I wanted to develop and I couldn't do it. I don't know the history of the head coach, but he has done very well.'

The injury merry-go-round was in full swing as the big Swede returned, but Liam Cooper only lasted a matter of minutes before injury forced the big Finn into action again. He may have been fresh from a successful debut, but this was Aapo Halme's baptism of fire, a totally different challenge. The home team started very well. Leeds couldn't get a foothold in the game and survived a huge scare when Sharp somehow bounced a free header over the bar from six yards. It was a great relief to get to half-time at 0-0.

I was watching alone in my lounge again, which of course can never generate the emotions of being at the game. I suppose the next best thing is being in a packed pub, which can imitate some feelings of being in the crowd; the chanting, the ranting and raving, the celebrating or the suffering, all as one. But it could never replicate the real thing; you are not a part of the event, you can't affect it, you can't smell it or feel it, and you can only see and hear what the TV allows. Watching at home on your own does have its advantages over the pub, with no one in your way, no distractions, and no worrying about where your next pint is coming from, just total concentration. Nowadays you can still discuss the game live with your mates over WhatsApp too, and today my mates were all in agreement; it was a matter of time before Sheffield United scored.

Leeds remained on the back foot in the second half, and survived another big scare when a mix-up at in defence presented an open goal to McGoldrick. Instead of stroking the ball into the net, the famously goal-shy striker opted to take a touch, allowing Peacock-Farrell to recover some ground. Now faced with a largely open goal, McGoldrick shot, but not at the open part, and the ball ricocheted off Peacock-Farrell's legs to safety. It was a shocking miss, but in the 82nd minute came something even more shocking – a Leeds United smash and grab! Under pressure, a dodgy back pass sent Sheffield United's goalkeeper, Dean Henderson, scampering wide of his goal. Unsure whether to clear the ball or control it, the loanee from our bitter rivals (just to make it all the sweeter) did a mixture of the two, which presented the ball to the Boy Wonder, Jack Clarke. With quick feet and astute awareness, the teenager put the chance on a plate for Pablo Hernández, who converted into the empty net to send the Leeds fans wild. I couldn't believe what I was seeing. Was this really Leeds? A team that can fluke victory in a vital away game? They still needed to see the job through, and with a strong backbone and the help of the crossbar Leeds held on.

This game was unique for Bielsa's team in that it was the first (and only) time all season that they didn't have the majority of possession. It was also their first win at Bramall Lane since the day Howard Wilkinson's men were crowned champions back in 1992, a stat that reflects how rarely Leeds have turned up in big away games in my lifetime, especially Yorkshire derbies. The record in the red half of Sheffield was so bad that my favourite visit was a dismal 2-0 defeat in 2005, thanks to a chance encounter with our shyster chairman in traffic on the way home. To my surprise he was willing to engage in a slanging match as I hurled abuse at him for selling Alan Smith to Manchester United, before the traffic thinned out and he sped off. Thankfully those dark days seemed confined to the past. El Loco had created a 'new Leeds', a world away from the 'typical Leeds' that a large chunk of our fans had only ever experienced.

Leeds United 2-1 Queens Park Rangers

Back to Elland Road, and today's opponents were a Steve McClaren side who had recovered from a disastrous start to the season and were suddenly closing in on the play-off zone. Emergency right-back Stuart Dallas was the latest casualty of the injury curse, so emergency midfielder Jamie Shackleton started as super-emergency right-back.

Despite QPR taking a shock lead, the Elland Road faithful remained faithful, something that could seldom be said in the pre-Bielsa days, and our patience was rewarded on the stroke of half-time. QPR's defence had been dropping deeper and deeper, and deep into injury time they were comically deep – all 11 QPR players were inside their own box when Hernández picked up the ball 20 yards out. The Spanish magician waved his magic wand, jinking past a defender then poking a genius pass through the eye of a needle for Kemar Roofe to equalise.

For the third game running Jack Clarke was introduced at half-time in place of the ineffective Jack Harrison, and his impact was again terrific. Shackleton was also having a really good game at full-back and the teenagers looked a fearsome combination down the right, in a partnership I hoped to see flourish over the next 15 years (but one I would never see again!). The winning goal felt inevitable, but not a soul in attendance could have predicted the circumstances in which it came – an incident that shocked Elland Road to its very core; Leeds were awarded a penalty! A contentious one, too. I had no idea whether it was a handball or not – I don't even think the ref knew – but my word, was this overdue! It had been 59 matches since Leeds's last penalty (which was missed). Roofe confidently grabbed the ball, and very confidently blasted it into the bottom corner. Hooray! Hoping to cause havoc in the penalty area, QPR brought on the giant former Leeds striker Matt Smith, but Bielsa responded in kind by bringing on Aapo Halme, who nullified Smith, and Leeds grabbed another pretty ugly victory.

But the ugly wins are pretty to me, and Bielsa's Leeds were showing a doggedness and desire to win that would not cease. Some not-so-great Leeds teams have had this same quality, but not only did Bielsa's team love defending, they were also hell-bent on winning the ball back as quickly as possible. I was hopeful the South American flair would soon return, that the attack would click and the goals would flow, but winning ugly will always have its own unique charm.

Bolton Wanderers 0-1 Leeds United

The Christmas period was upon us, commencing with a short trip across the Pennines. Bolton had stayed up miraculously last season, but after a promising start this time around they were now in a slump, with serious financial issues that would continue to escalate.

In the lead-up to this game Leeds's playing squad was dealt another major blow as Samu Sáiz had requested a move back to Spain; his partner was pregnant and they wanted to be close to family after a difficult previous pregnancy. The request was granted and Bielsa removed him from the squad immediately. Sáiz had played his last game for Leeds. I swayed between seething and philosophical about the club's accommodation of this request. On the one hand, he wasn't in the team, hadn't scored all season, and wasn't reaching the levels we saw when he first arrived in Yorkshire, but on the other hand, the Championship is a long and gruelling season, so losing a player of Sáiz's calibre was a big loss whether he was currently in form or not. The consolation prize was the injury merry-go-round bringing Patrick Bamford back after three months on the sidelines. Bamford had recently scored a 'worldie' in training that had Bielsa running half the length of the pitch to hug and congratulate his marquee signing. The incident was caught on camera and caused an internet sensation, so of course Bielsa was questioned about it afterwards: 'It was a spontaneous reaction to a beautiful goal. I allowed myself this excess.'

I was forced to listen on the radio for the first time this season, something I always try to avoid. As a child I was convinced I cursed Leeds by listening on the radio – and who could disagree, the evidence was damning! When I had my first season ticket, in 1992/93, Leeds were the reigning champions of England and had the best home record in the country, losing only once at Elland Road all season. I was too young to go to away games so the only option was to listen on the radio, and Leeds went the whole season without winning a single away match. And I listened to every miserable one. My happiest memory of listening on the radio was in 1997, when Nigel Martyn saved an injury-time penalty in the FA Cup third round at Selhurst Park, but even that only salvaged a draw.

This match was a real slog in awful conditions, and every time Popey and Noel Whelan complained on the radio about the weather, I couldn't help imagining the wry smile on Sáiz's face as he quaffed Rioja back in Madrid. At half-time the teams were locked at 0-0, so Bielsa again brought on Jack Clarke and, a little later, Patrick Bamford. As I sat on my bed I experienced a rare bout of optimism. I really fancied Bamford to score. He had already scored against Bolton this season (in the League Cup first round), was banging them in for the reserves, and simply deserved a bit of luck.

Suddenly Leeds were on the counterattack and Clarke carried the ball 40 yards up the pitch before squaring to Klich, who in turn squared it to Pablo Hernández. With his Spanish comrade already back in Madrid, Pablo now needed to deliver all the magic for this team, and he made the perfect start by slipping the ball through the defender's legs perfectly into the path of Bamford, who swept a lovely controlled finish low inside the near post. Bamford sprinted down the touchline to celebrate with the physios who had nursed him back to fitness, his beaming smile a joy to behold, with the Leeds fans in the background going loco.

Yet again it was backs to the wall for the closing stages, and with only one six-foot defender available Leeds were vulnerable. Bolton had a strong penalty claim dismissed, but there were no other heart-stopping moments as the late aerial bombardment was dealt with admirably once again. With five victories on the bounce Leeds were now within striking distance of table-topping Norwich, and by the time the next game kicked off they knew that victory would hand them the notorious Christmas number one spot.

Aston Villa 2-3 Leeds United

It was Sunday, 23 December, and with none of my mates working Christmas Eve the plan was to make a day of it, but that was kiboshed by all-encompassing hangovers. We were quite naive to make such a plan as the previous night was the last Saturday before Christmas, the biggest night out of the year. Everyone was out, spirits were high and spirits were flowing, and when Leeds boxer Josh Warrington successfully defended his IBF world title, there was no stopping the merriment. My last memory of the night was bouncing in a five-man huddle outside Monty's, singing the line 'All I want for Christmas is yoooooooouuu baby!' over and over again. I can't remember stopping singing it. So it was armchairs all round for the biggest match of the season so far.

Like our Mariah Carey tribute, the injury merry-go-round seemed never-ending. Last week's hero, Patrick Bamford, had cruelly suffered another knee injury and would miss a further two months, but Luke Ayling was back ahead of schedule, and straight into the team. There was a further twist just before kick-off when Barry Douglas injured himself in the warm-up, so Leif Davis was thrust from the youth team into the starting 11 for his senior debut. Understandably, Leeds made a shaky start. They had already survived an early scare when a long ball caused confusion at the back and Villa pounced to take the lead. Then another mistake, Villa pounced again and suddenly Leeds were 2-0 down. Could this hangover get any worse? Leeds fought back impressively and controlled the rest of the first half, cutting through Villa's own makeshift defence time and again, without converting any of the chances. Discussing over WhatsApp at half-time, my mates and Dad all agreed that one goal could turn this game on its head.

There are three things certain in life; death, taxes, and Jack Clarke replacing the ineffective Jack Harrison for the second half. This time playing from the left, the teenager set about tearing Egypt captain Ahmed Elmohamady apart. The first time the ball was played out to him, Clarke controlled it with a majestic touch on the outside of his right foot and headed towards the penalty area. His dragged stepover was becoming trademark, but on this occasion it went wrong and the ball trickled out of play to sarcastic cheers. Undeterred, the second time he got the ball he set about his task again. Elmohamady backed off and backed off, but instead of going for the line, this time Clarke cut inside and whipped a beautiful shot into the far corner of the net, giving the keeper no chance. There was nothing sarcastic about the cheers now. Despite having just scored his first career goal in front of more than 40,000 fans, with millions more watching at home, and Christmas around the corner, Boy Wonder wasn't in celebratory mood. Instead, he pointed instructions for Roofe to retrieve the ball and shouted encouragement to the rest of his team-mates. The comeback was on.

Leeds's tails were really wagging now and they were bossing the game thanks in no small part to the centre-back pairing. Kalvin Phillips was still covering for Liam Cooper and playing magnificently again, always one step ahead of the attackers, always in complete control. Alongside him, Pontus Jansson was having one of his best Leeds games, and cometh the hour Pontus was the man who commethed up with the equaliser, in brilliant circumstances. Pablo was preparing to take a corner when a Leeds fan invaded the pitch. Jansson, already up for the corner, sprinted back to the halfway line to usher the adoring fan off the pitch, then made his way back into the box, attacked the corner with gusto, and powered an unstoppable header into the corner. Not all superheroes wear capes. 'GET IN THERE, PONTUS!' I was jumping around the living room, headache pounding, but I couldn't care less.

The rest of the game was a pulsating, end-to-end affair. As injury time started, both teams were still going for the win, and with a minute remaining Leeds got a throw-in deep in their own half. I was hoping they would waste the last few seconds and hoof it away from goal, but the players stayed true to Bielsa's philosophy, passing calmly out of defence before swinging the ball out to Shackleton, who had come on for Ayling and had bags of energy to sprint with the ball up the right wing. He wasn't the only one as Alioski was soon providing the overlap and Roofe and Clarke were sprinting upfield too. Shack passed to Alioski, whose deep cross was poor, but the defensive header was poorer still and the ball bobbled to the corner of the box, where it was met by the assured left boot of Kemar Roofe. 'Roooofe… WINS IT! Right. At the very. Last!' I didn't hear the commentary at the time, of course, but I've heard it a hundred times since. The celebrations were as wild in my living room as they were on the pitch, in the stands, and in homes and pubs all across Yorkshire. Leeds had done it, a mindblowing, miraculous victory. We were in dreamland, a Christmas wonderland, a Bielsa wonderland!

After the game Frankie and I headed into town. Leeds were top of the pops at Christmas and everyone in Harrogate seemed so happy, none more so than me. Hangover, what hangover? When I got home I spent the rest of the night watching the highlights, fan videos, anything I could of the match. I wasn't going to be sleeping; I was still bouncing off the walls. Capping it all off was an incredible stat I saw on Twitter; every Leeds player on the pitch in the second half was already at the club when Marcelo Bielsa arrived. For Leeds to be able to reach the levels they did at Villa Park, with no additions to a squad that struggled so poorly last season, is beyond superlatives. It must be one of the most dramatic coaching feats in world football. Bielsa had transformed everything.

Leeds United 3-2 Blackburn Rovers

Come Boxing Day I was still buzzing from the win at Villa Park, buzzing but ill. I had to bail on the pre-match drinks with Lewis and George, but there was no way I was going to miss the game, of course. I promised Frankie I'd wrap up warm and just stand and watch, no shouting or chanting, though in the back of my head I knew this was going to be a stretch, even if we got the nice easy 3-0 win our nervous systems longed for.

With Lewis living in Montreal and George in London with his young family, trips to Elland Road together were few and far between. In fact, this was the first time the three of us had been together at Elland Road since we played on the hallowed turf in May 2012. The club used to stage matches at the end of the season, when £200 got you a place in the team, a full kit, and a DVD of the game. It was money well spent and the day couldn't have gone any better. I had met Frankie at a wedding the previous Saturday and we had been messaging each other since. The night before the game she told me to 'play like Messi', so when I latched on to Lewis's 40-yard through ball I produced a trademark Messi finish, dinking majestically over the keeper to open the scoring. In the second half I laid on an assist for Lewis, then in the last minute, with the team hanging on to a 2-1 lead, I sent George clean through and he buried it at the Kop end. What a euphoric feeling it was when the ball hit the net; all three of us had scored, the perfect end to a magical day. I immediately hung up my boots and still proudly boast an Elland Road goal involvement ratio that may never be beaten.

In his weekly *Leeds, Leeds, Leeds!* Facebook post, my dad said he had never seen a comeback like the Villa game before, nor would he see another in his lifetime. Well he was wrong about the first bit as he was with me at Elland Road in November 1997 when Leeds fought back from 3-0 down to beat Jim Smith's Derby County 4-3 with a last-minute Lee Bowyer goal. And the very next week we were at Oakwell together, soaked to the bone in pouring rain, as Leeds recovered from being 2-0 down to beat Barnsley 3-2 with a late Derek Lilley goal. My dad successfully recalled the Barnsley game once I'd reminded him of the 'Belly Buster' pre-match hot sandwich. He had seen such comebacks before, and he would see such comebacks again.

There was no sign of a post-Villa or Christmas hangover as Leeds set about their task with great enthusiasm, but for all the pressure there was little goalmouth action. At this point I had accepted this was the way it was going to be; slowly grinding teams down rather than blowing them away. Leeds had only held half-time leads twice in the last 19 matches, but the law of averages would start to even out today thanks to an own goal following good work by Jack Harrison. My boss, Chris, has a phobia of 1-0 half-time leads and prefers to go in level or behind, rather than 1-0 up. He says it affects the momentum of the match and that once the momentum is lost you cannot get it back. It may sound crazy, and it comes from the only football fan I've ever met who is more pessimistic than myself but, like my radio phobia, if you judge the theory by Leeds's results you couldn't really argue. Had they led in 17 of the last 19 games instead of chasing them, perhaps they wouldn't be top?

Chris's words were ringing in my head when a rash challenge from Ayling resulted in a penalty to Blackburn and the equaliser. The precious half-time lead had lasted two minutes – could Leeds regain the momentum? It was a struggle, and just as the game looked to be heading for a dull 1-1 draw, Blackburn won a free kick, at least 30 yards from goal. The free kick beat the wall and somehow beat Peacock-Farrell too, who could only help the ball into the net. What would have been a disappointing draw was now looking like a back-down-to-earth crashing defeat.

Pontus was sent up front (or sent himself up front) and Leeds, for the first time this season, went route one. With the first attack, almost straight from the kick-off, a cross from the right was flicked on at the near post, Jansson stooped low to head it into the bottom corner, but the keeper made a flying save. The rebound fell to Hernández, and from a tight angle he side-footed it into the top corner, but the keeper made a flying save. The rebound fell to Roofe, and from an awkward height he powered it down the middle, but the keeper made a flying save. Or did he? The Leeds players were celebrating, the referee was checking his goal-line technology, and Elland Road erupted when he swung his arm towards the centre circle, signalling 'goal' in a theatrical manner Mike Dean would have been proud of.

For most teams, equalising in injury time means 'game saved', but for Bielsa's Leeds it means 'game on'. With injury time running out Leeds got a free kick wide on the right, almost the same spot that had brought the equaliser. As Barry Douglas trotted over to take it, Elland Road was trembling with excitement. I unbuttoned my coat, knowing that if we scored I would lose the last of my buttons, having already lost the other, but Douglas couldn't beat the first man. Elland Road exhaled. Forshaw picked up the loose ball and some idiots still had it in them to shout 'Shoooooooot!', but Forshaw is not an idiot, and instead played a nice crisp pass out to Pablo Hernández, free on the right wing. Pablo controlled it with his first touch, gently caressed it with his second touch, and with his third touch swung in the most sumptuous of crosses straight on to the head of Roofe, who planted a bullet header into the bottom corner of the net, sending Elland Road into complete pandemonium!

I couldn't believe what I was seeing and fell backwards over my seat as my immune system sighed and shut down. Pontus Jansson stormed around the pitch as if he'd scored himself, before collapsing on his front and banging the ground in disbelief. He briefly raised his head and glanced at the Kop to make sure it was really happening. It was! The rest of the players were embracing in the north-west corner, while the dugout was going potty too, especially Gaetano Berardi, who was carrying translator Salim Lamrani around the technical area with one arm, while punching the air like a madman with the other. There was one man, however, who wasn't celebrating. Marcelo Bielsa was marching down the touchline, shouting and pointing at his players to get back into position. There was still a job to do, and still a minute to go. He even raised his hand in apology to the Blackburn bench when realising he'd encroached into their technical area. What an incredible man.

The final whistle blew and the lap of honour was joyous. Our heroes had done it again. Was there anything they couldn't do? For the first time in Leeds's 100-year history we had won having trailed in injury time, extending the winning sequence to a club record-equalling seven league games. Emotions were running high on the way back to the car, and sharing this sensational experience with Lewis and George made it even more special. What magic occurs when we come together at Elland Road! These two Christmas miracles would never be forgotten, not even by my dad, but this time it was quite possible he would never see the likes again.

Leeds United 0-2 Hull City

The team that tops the Championship at Christmas always goes up automatically; at least they had done for the last ten years. This type of stat really annoys me due to my respect for the law of averages. Surely the longer the sequence, the more likely it will break? Past events held no relevance anyway; Leeds still had to collect as many points again otherwise they wouldn't go up, no matter if they were top at Christmas, New Year, or even Easter. My dad sided with the statisticians, inflaming my annoyance by claiming they couldn't fail from here. When it was put to Bielsa in his pre-match press conference, I was a little disappointed he didn't pull a grenade out of his pocket, or at least explain why the stat was a load of rubbish. El Loco remained unfazed: 'Let's not be the ones to break the sequence.'

For the first time in a generation, my dad drove me and Lewis to the game, as he had done throughout the David O'Leary years. It was quite funny really. On the way home my dad and I would always order pizza from Big Mamma's, where it was three for the price of two. In all the years that we took Lewis home (probably 100 times), we never once offered him the free pizza; my dad and I would always share it. It's worth pointing out that Lewis's drop off point was before the pizza shop, but we really didn't have to rub it in his face by making him order for us!

After reflecting on the Blackburn game, talk quickly turned to the main event, Lewis's debut at Park Fisheries. Everyone we had taken had rated it ten out of ten, and of course we fully expected the same today. All seemed well as we took our place in the 'restaurant' outside, with the tabby cat (aka the waiter) sniffing around for donations as usual, but, to our dismay, the standard had slipped for the first time. My dad and I still finished ours, of course, but Lewis shared his fish with the waiter and his chips with the bin. Possibly some form of Stockholm syndrome.

Despite Hull's good form coming into this game, we arrived at Elland Road fully expecting to witness a club record eighth successive victory, and Leeds were in full control until Kalvin Phillips's rare mistake gifted the red-hot Jarrod Bowen with the opening goal. In the second half Leeds huffed and puffed, the crowd waited and hoped, but when Bowen struck again it knocked the stuffing out of us. The players continued to huff and puff, the fans continued to hope, but deep down we all knew The Lord Mayor's Show ended on Boxing Day, and Leeds fell to their fourth defeat of the season.

So no club record for Bielsa, but his team remained top of the league and there was no reason to panic. But I just couldn't help myself. I started to pick apart the seven-game winning run; three were decided in injury time, one was decided by a goalkeeping howler. Were Leeds in a false position? The fact that they had dominated every game was irrelevant in my scrambled head. Then I turned to the fixture list and noticed that, out of the current top six, Leeds had only played Middlesbrough at home. To any normal person this would seem positive; everyone still has to come to Elland Road, and the toughest away games were nearly all out of the way. Yet I managed to turn this on its head; were Leeds only top because of all the home wins against relegation fodder? In the second half of the season there would be few of those easier home games and the team would be tested on a new level. Could they cope? I was going out of my mind and it wasn't even January.

January 2019

1	**Leeds**	**51**
2	Norwich City	48
3	West Brom	46
4	Sheffield United	44
4	Middlesbrough	42
6	Derby County	42

Nottingham Forest 4-2 Leeds United

A televised fixture with a 3pm kick-off? It could only be New Year's Day, the day when nobody knows what day it is. Despite Forest still being within touching distance of the play-off places, rumours were rife that Aitor Karanka would be sacked if they lost to Leeds. I felt this was a good sign – maybe the Forest players would be happy to see the back of their manager and give Bielsa's men an easy ride. Then again, this was Leeds they were up against.

Karanka's men got off to the best possible start thanks to Adam Forshaw's underhit back-pass. Jack Colback latched on to the ball ahead of the hesitant Peacock-Farrell, rounded the keeper and tapped it home. New year, new predictable old Leeds? Frustration turned to anger when Jack Harrison was hauled down as he raced clean through on goal; it was a stonewall red card, but the referee shied away from the correct decision and only gave a yellow. I was fuming. My anger was compounded when Phillips lost control of the ball and made a desperate and unsuccessful lunge to win it back. Despite there being no malice or danger to the opponent, in the 'modern game' it was a red card and this time the referee didn't shy away from the correct decision – what a surprise. Leeds were a man down when they should have been a man up.

My mates had come round for the game and at half-time the atmosphere in the kitchen was despondent. No amount of nibbles could cheer us up. However, in young Jack Clarke hope springs eternal, and once again he was brought on for Harrison as Leeds made clear what their intentions would be – to win the game, the same as always. The ten men took the game to Forest, and the equaliser came just five minutes after the restart, through Boy Wonder. Not content with that, ten-man Leeds kept piling forward, and ten minutes later they took the lead when Pontus headed across goal to Alioski for what should have been a tap-in. Alioski, in his excitable-like-a-puppy-at-Christmas nature, lashed at the ball on the volley as hard as he could, and had he been three yards out he would have skied it, but thankfully he was only two yards out and sliced it into the roof of the net. Wild celebrations in my kitchen, and wild celebrations in the away end, where Berardi and Salim Lamrani were on the front row and practically invaded the pitch as the Leeds players huddled around them. It was brilliant to see; fans and players fused into one.

Still not content, the ten men continued to pile forward. Forest were on the ropes and Leeds were going for the jugular, but five minutes later they were caught on the counterattack and it was 2-2. The game was now resembling a basketball match as, straight from kick-off, Pantilimon pulled off a brilliant save to deny Roofe, then Forest went up the other end, won a corner, and made it 3-2. Then in the blink of an eye it was 4-2 after another counterattack and another clinical finish.

Three goals in seven minutes and the game was over. Except it wasn't over, or it might not have been as Leeds continued to make chance after chance, but there were no more goals, thus Marcelo Bielsa tasted successive defeats for the first time in England.

With the benefit of hindsight, some fans pointed the finger of blame at Bielsa for not shutting up shop at 2-1. The Great Man explained that he had considered bringing on a defender, but the attackers were playing so well he didn't want to bring any of them off and lose the impetus. Fine by me. The way Leeds played with ten men underlined how much I loved El Loco and his team, and, despite another defeat, I felt calmer than I did before the game. In this moment promotion didn't seem quite as important as having Bielsa here, though deep down I knew promotion mattered more *because* Bielsa was here. Leeds needed to do it for him; this was to be his masterpiece. He deserved it as much as our long-suffering fans.

Leeds United 2-0 Derby County

It's a rare occasion when my mates come to a game en masse. Nowadays it's basically an annual event, and this year we delayed our Christmas do to coincide with the Derby game. Not because of the opposition, I should add. At this level they hardly matter, you barely notice them. There are some exceptions – league position may be one, whether the away fans will travel in numbers may be another. Significant opposition is one thing I miss about the Premier League as historical issues with clubs and banter with individual players are rare in the Championship. Come to think of it, Derby actually ticked all of the above boxes; up near the top of the table, travel in numbers, a historic rivalry, and Lampard in the dugout, who's Chelsea links are enough to consider him a rival despite having only made a handful of appearances at Elland Road.

Nevertheless, my mates weren't here for Derby County, they were here for Bielsa's Leeds and a Friday night piss-up.

I booked the afternoon off work and warmed up in Harrogate with pints, pool, and Sambucas, before heading to Leeds to join up with the rest of the lads. For reasons previously mentioned, I was controlling my drunkenness, refusing any more shots once the evening drew in, and when things started to get messy The Woollards and I jumped in a taxi to the ground. En route, Frankie, of all people, broke one of the biggest stories of the season to me, reporting that Bielsa had sent a spy to Derby's training ground to gather intelligence ahead of the game. I messaged her back saying Bielsa would never do anything underhand, he was a beacon of fair play. As usual, we were both right.

Elland Road under the lights is special. I don't know why or how, but floodlights do special things to special football stadiums, and the atmosphere was electric. Sky would claim that the Derby players were affected by the pre-match controversy, but that was nonsense; their startled and meek performance was due to the ferocity of the support and relentless nature of the Leeds team. They raced out of the blocks at 100mph and opened the scoring midway through the first half when Jack Clarke – finally making his first league start – picked up a loose ball on the edge of the box, gained half a yard on the full-back and drilled a superb low ball into the corridor of uncertainty. Kemar Roofe met the ball with a flick of his right boot, sending it flying into the top corner with a fantastic finish.

At half-time I was too delirious to worry about Chris's theory, but just like the last time Leeds held the dreaded 1-0 half-time lead, it only lasted two minutes. This time, Clarke got the ball and skinned the full-back again, his looping cross wasn't dealt with by the keeper and Harrison was on hand to fire home from two yards. There was still a whole half to go, so despite the 2-0 lead I was nervous and clock-watching, but there was no need as it remained men against boys for the rest of the match. Pontus and the returning Cooper were impeccable at the back, Forshaw and Klich so dominant in midfield. I had recently wondered why Kalvin Phillips couldn't get into the England team; now I was wondering how he would get back into the Leeds team! The final whistle put Derby out of their misery and Leeds had bounced back from successive defeats with the performance of the season. Elland Road was buzzing.

Sky's post-match coverage was dominated by the 'spying' incident. In his post-match interview Bielsa took full responsibility, admitting he had sent a young intern to Derby's training ground, a tactic that was not against the rules and common everywhere else he had managed. This really should have been the end of it, and the EFL's response to Derby's complaint could have been as simple as, 'Put a fence up if you want private training sessions.' As I lay awake in bed, too excited to sleep, I was pleased the attention was being deflected away from such a masterly performance by Leeds, and the prodigious man of the match, Jack Clarke. At this stage I had no idea how big 'Spygate' would become.

Spygate

The next day, alarm bells started ringing. The EFL announced they would be investigating Derby's complaint, concerned that Leeds had broken a rule that was introduced at the start of the season: 'All clubs should act in good faith towards each other.' It was hard not to surmise that the governing body had dug really deep to be able to take this further. There was no rule against observing training sessions, but this vague and obscure rule gave them the opportunity to wage war on

Leeds United, and the media threw all their heavy artillery behind them.

The week following the outstanding victory over Derby was pretty much beyond belief. Spygate was front- and back-page news and every man and his dog had an opinion on it. Most respected pundits either laughed it off, said it was normal, or said it was clever, and the rest wanted Bielsa's head on a spike (or just wanted to get themselves some airtime). Some of the comments were ludicrous, and verging on xenophobic if we're going to get all uppity about it. Peter Shilton's take, live on Sky Sports News, summed up the witch hunt perfectly. After talking the normal rubbish about 'not wanting to see that in the English game', he exposed his lack of expertise in comical fashion by referring to Bielsa as 'Italian'. When he was corrected about Bielsa actually being Argentinian, Shilton replied, 'Oh, is he? That makes it even worse then, doesn't it?' The icing on the cake was André Villas-Boas admitting that he 'spied' regularly while at Chelsea, where the team's vice-captain was, of course, Derby manager Frank Lampard!

Halfway through the week, Bielsa called a press conference at an hour's notice, and some of the media were reporting 'on good authority' that Bielsa was resigning. The Leeds United fanbase went into meltdown. The man had turned the club on its head; the first team were top of the Championship, the reserve team were top of their league, and the youth team were top of their league. It would be the biggest travesty since the 1975 European Cup Final if this out-of-control media circus brought a premature end to the Bielsa era. My heart was in my mouth. I was so angry and worried. It was one of the most horrible feelings I can remember in football.

What transpired would go down in folklore, a 90-minute PowerPoint presentation during which The Great Man revealed the astonishing depth of his pre-match preparations. It was extraordinary. He laid bare his vast research for the Derby match as an example, which had taken 328 hours' work. After four hours of analyses for each of their 31 games this season, and 51 games last season, Bielsa knew more about Derby than Lampard himself. It would not have been intentional, but I loved the thought of how riled Derby would have been by this, especially as hard copies of the presentation were left on a table for the journalists to take home too. El Loco had literally laid out the full dossier on them!

Bielsa's intention was to accelerate the EFL's investigation by explaining, rather than justifying, his actions, and to defend his honour. Bielsa argued that no competitive advantage could be gained from viewing a training session, but his anxiety compells him to leave no stone unturned. He used his own side's weaknesses as a perfect example: 'We already know everything about our opponents' set-piece drills, and still we concede half our goals from set pieces,' leading The Great Man to his grand finale. 'All this information is useless. Why do I do it? Because I am stupid.' It was a comical ending, but the point was that Leeds were not winning because of the research, and certainly not because of 'spying'. Such an accusation was an insult to the hard work of everyone at the club. I felt blessed to have been able to watch the full presentation on Twitter. It was a masterclass. We all loved Bielsa already – the Leeds fans will never be more united than under his stewardship – but this episode truly pushed him into legendary status at Elland Road.

The journalists in attendance were in awe of Bielsa's methods, but the next morning the media circus went into overdrive. The gutter press ran front pages with moronic headlines and pictures of Bielsa dressed as Austin Powers or Dr Evil, and the gutter pundits continued their ignorant drivel. On talkSPORT, Dean Saunders explained that all coaches do analysis and what Bielsa does is no different to what he did as a non-league manager, using two students from the local college. I normally find it easy to ignore the rubbish on talkSPORT as, after all, the opinions are mostly aired to entertain, drive conversation, and ultimately sell advertising space, but Bielsa takes notice of everything written about him, so it really upset me that he was under such an attack. I was totally ashamed of our country.

Stoke City 2-1 Leeds United

Matchday, and finally an escape from the media circus. It was my first away game of the season and another flashback to yesteryear, driving to the game with Paul, who had travelled with me home and away in years gone by. Paul lived in Holland now, and considering he was blind drunk at the Derby game, this was his first time seeing Bielsa's Leeds in the flesh.

Like all Leeds fans, I love away days. The excitement of invading enemy lines, the adventure of visiting new towns and stadiums, the sheer pride of being among our phenomenal travelling fans. Away games were once the be-all and end-all for me, and there was a period when I had an away season ticket instead of a home one, but in recent years they had become a rarity. Once through the turnstiles at Stoke I realised what I'd been missing. I was wide-eyed at the scene that greeted me. Underneath the stand had always been fun – boozy antics and lots of singing – but I couldn't remember it ever being as fervent as this. It was jam-packed, you could barely move, yet everyone was moving, bouncing up and down, throwing beers around, and singing on repeat, 'Bielsa he comes from Argentina, he came to manage Super Leeds. They call him El Loco cos he's crazy, but he knows exactly what we need… JANSSON AT THE BACK, BAMFORD IN ATTACK, Leeds are going to the Premier League!'

Once out in the winter sun there was an emotional moment as, credit to Stoke, the whole stadium rose to honour the memory of Toby Nye, a young Leeds fan who had tragically lost his battle with cancer in the week before the game. The support of the club, especially Liam Cooper, during Toby's illness was truly admirable. I can only hope it brought some comfort to the family. It must have done for Toby.

Within minutes of kick-off it was clear that Stoke were nothing to fear, but my only worry was falling victim to the 'new manager bounce'. Nathan Jones had recently been poached from Luton Town, so Bielsa had watched every Luton match, as well as every Stoke match, in preparation for today. Impressive dedication, but no different to what Dean Saunders would have done as manager of Crawley Town, obviously. Leeds controlled the first half without causing too many problems for Stoke, who themselves could only lump aimless balls forward that were dealt with easily. In truth, it was a poor half of football, but the three points were there for the taking.

In the second half the game turned on a dreadful defensive error by Klich that gifted Stoke the lead, and an outrageous call by the referee then turned the game further away from Leeds. A long ball in behind the defence was latched on to by Benik Afobe, ahead of Pontus Jansson, who tumbled to the floor as Afobe shrugged off his challenge. Now bearing down on goal, Afobe's next touch was too heavy, and Peacock-Farrell rushed out to make a very good save. However, the preposterous referee pulled the game back, awarded a free kick to Stoke, and sent Jansson off! It was a bizarre decision, one of many on the day (in the first half he had marched a Leeds defensive wall back 15 paces, rather than the industry-standard ten).

Leeds still came agonisingly close to equalising when Ayling's powerful header was miraculously saved by Jack

Butland, but soon after that Stoke killed the game off on the counterattack. Alioski's 95th-minute goal was scant consolation; it was now three defeats in four games for Leeds (four in five if you include a severely weakened team losing at QPR in the FA Cup). 'We arrived easily to the final third but could not convert possession into dangerous actions,' said Bielsa, and as always he was spot on. Leeds's failures in the final third were becoming as worrying as they were frustrating.

Leeds were still two points clear at the top but it was impossible not to wonder whether the wheels were coming off, especially after a vivid dream I woke up from later in the week. I dreamt I was driving my car with Bielsa in the passenger seat when another car crashed into us (Spygate?). At first everything seemed okay and we continued on as normal (beating Derby?), but soon I could hear an awful noise (the media?), so we pulled over to inspect the car and saw that one of the wheels had come off (oh shit!).

Rotherham United 1-2 Leeds United

It was another manic week at Leeds United and Spygate just wouldn't go away. Rival clubs were now calling for a points deduction, and half the league signed a letter to the EFL demanding a full investigation. The EFL were already investigating, so this letter, and the fact the EFL released it to the press two hours before kick-off at Stoke, really boiled my blood. Again, it was nice to have the distraction of an actual football match, but there was immense pressure on Leeds going into this game. Rotherham were destined for relegation so there would be no glory in victory and no excuse in defeat – Leeds simply had to get three points on the board.

The merry-go-round delivered Phillips back from suspension to cover for the suspended Jansson, and there was a debut for Leeds's first signing of the January transfer window, Kiko Casilla. It may have been a free transfer but this was a high-profile signing as Casilla was joining from Real Madrid where he had won three successive Champions League titles, albeit as substitute keeper. I felt for Peacock-Farrell as, despite how it may sound, I did rate him. He had good hands, good feet, a good mentality, was a good talker and a good reader of the game, but when a goalkeeper's weakness is shot-stopping you have a problem. I was happy we invested time in him, but happier that we replaced him, and a treble Champions League winner would do nicely. It was an impressive move from the director of football, Victor Orta, whose reputation at Leeds had transformed in parallel with the team. In his first season Orta had brought in a raft of pointless or substandard players from abroad, but learnt quickly from those mistakes and was instrumental in bringing Marcelo Bielsa to the club. For that alone we will all be eternally grateful.

The first half was not at all pretty as Leeds just couldn't get going and Rotherham took a deserved lead when some random turned into Steven Gerrard again. Casilla had no chance of saving the fantastic long-range drive, so his first job for Leeds was picking the ball out of the net. At half-time I was extremely stressed. Defeat today would trigger full-blown panic stations, especially with games against Norwich and Middlesbrough up next. I spent the break WhatsApping my mates, mainly complaining about Mateusz Klich, willing Bielsa to give him a rest, though not in such kind words. WhatsApp is an important outlet for letting off steam and you have to be able to vent your anger. Football is an emotional release, after all, and that's why we love it. I even love being outraged, when all is said and done. Of course, I would never reduce myself to directly abusing players like some do over social media. This I will never understand.

Although I was overreacting, Klich certainly wasn't at the top of his game and hadn't scored since October (ironically since his 'Klich is scoring goooaaals' chant took off), so when the equaliser came it was inevitably Klich who got it. A speculative forward ball somehow created confusion between defender and goalkeeper, and the lovable Pole nipped in to poke it into the net, sending the Leeds fans behind the goal potty. 'IT, COULD, BE, 20 yards or 30 yards, everywhere we go.' I immediately messaged my mates, 'Roofe is shite,' but I needn't have bothered as I'd already tempted fate enough.

In the 86th minute some nice football on the edge of the box found Klich in space, where he shuffled across the area to open up even more space, then calmly passed the ball into the net, sending the Leeds fans behind the goal pottier still. 'Forty yards or 50 yards, Klich is scoring gooooaaaaals, Klich is scoring goooaaaaals!' The last few minutes were a nervy affair, with long balls and long throws raining into the Leeds box. It was turning into a memorable debut for Casilla as he had already made a magnificent flying save to deny Rotherham the lead at 1-1, and now he was charging around trying to claim anything and everything that came into his area. I liked his confidence, but it wasn't good for the heart rate.

At the final whistle I bounced giddily around my bedroom and was thrilled with the victory, however it had come. The reaction from El Loco was very different. I had never seen him so emotional as he shared a long hug with one of his coaches, embracing like they would never see each other again. The Great Man had really gone through the wringer in the last couple of weeks, not to mention the last 90 minutes, and it was moving to see how much it was taking out of him. God bless Marcelo.

February 2019

1	**Leeds**	**57**
2	Norwich City	54
3	West Brom	53
4	Sheffield United	51
5	Middlesbrough	47
6	Bristol City	47

Leeds United 1-3 Norwich City

The transfer window 'slammed shut' without any further additions to the Leeds squad, but that doesn't begin to tell the story. With Sáiz gone (and Lewis Baker too, if that makes any difference), Bielsa had identified the need for another attacking option, and Victor Orta quickly identified young Swansea winger Dan James as the primary target. By deadline day everything was agreed so James drove up to Elland Road, completed his medical, recorded his (now obligatory) welcome video, and waited for the final documents to come through from Swansea. But all was not well in South Wales and, amid boardroom wrangling and the sale of other key players, chairman Huw Jenkins refused to sign off the deal, defying the instructions of the club owners. The lack of response from Swansea caused panic at Elland Road and James even called his team-mates, pleading for their help to get it over the line, but 11pm passed and the deal was off. Leeds have been specialists at missing out on transfers in my lifetime, but I've never known a signing to get quite so close and still fall through. This was a bitter pill to swallow, and surely a clear breach of the sacred 'good faith' rule!

There were two special occasions rolled into one on the first Saturday of February; a top-of-the-table clash under the lights at Elland Road, and Paddy's 30th birthday. The event caught the imagination and a coachload of us headed to Headingley for a day session (no fish and chips *again* for daddy), though pre-match jitters were lingering behind the merriment for me. There was a long way to go in the promotion race and nothing would be decided tonight, but this was a huge opportunity for Leeds to take a giant leap towards the Premier League as victory would open up a six-point lead at the top. I still wasn't sure whether Norwich were a great side or just on a great run, and deep down, below my jitters, I expected another glorious night for the mighty whites.

Roared on by a passionate home crowd, Leeds started on the front foot, but it was the visitors who struck first from a cruelly deflected free kick with just five minutes on the clock. The nightmare start. Leeds responded superbly but Norwich repelled half an hour of incessant attacks and then then doubled their lead thanks to another cruel deflection that left Teemu Pukki with the easiest goal of a prolific season. The 2-0 half-time deficit was disastrous, but the atmosphere around Elland Road remained defiant. This was not 'typical Leeds' and everybody knew they could turn the game around.

What followed was the worst half of the season to date. The players looked drained and desperate as Norwich ran rings around them, and it was horrible to see. When Norwich scored their third goal (another bloody deflection), Leeds's fate was sealed. Bamford came on for what felt like his third debut, and having scored on his actual debut and his long-awaited return at Bolton, he completed the hat-trick with an injury-time header that consoled nobody.

It was a bitterly disappointing night. Not only had Leeds been knocked off the top of the league but their main promotion rival had come to Elland Road and played them off the park. Leeds had now lost more games in five weeks than they had in the whole first half of the season, and The Great Man's analysis did nothing to quell fans' fears. 'We need too many chances to score. We have lost the defensive solidity. This is an indication that the team is not doing well right now.' A tough trip to Middlesbrough was next, and desperate times call for desperate measures.

Middlesbrough 1-1 Leeds United

My previous two trips to The Riverside were in the home end with my favourite Smoggy, Tom. Both times Leeds lost 3-0, although at the end of the first drubbing I was cheering along with Tom as my pre-match bet – 3-0, Nugent first scorer – had come in for over £500. The second drubbing was a horrible Paul Heckingbottom experience in sub-zero temperatures. Keen to avoid an unwanted hat-trick I fled the country, arranging a work trip to Belgium that doubled up as a long weekend with Frankie.

On the Friday night, with Sheffield United leading 3-0 at Aston Villa, Leeds were on the verge of dropping out of the automatic promotion places for the first time since November. I'd been keeping half an eye on the score while supping lovely Belgian beers, and just as we left the bar to return to the hotel Villa pulled a goal back. There were only a few minutes left so I didn't hold any hope, but by the time we got back to our room Villa had scored again. Now I was excited and quickly loaded Sky Go, just in time to see Sheffield United crumble as Villa made it 3-3 deep into injury time. What a start to the weekend!

I had no way of watching or listening to the game, so I decided to switch off my phone and give myself a break from the promotion race. Surprisingly, the plan worked well. I felt completely liberated and we had a lovely day exploring the charming city of Bruges. However, as full time was approaching, my anxiety was rising. We were driving back to the airport and I was glued to the clock. I expected the game to finish at around 3.55pm local time, so waited until 4pm before pulling off the motorway to check the final score. As I loaded the Sky Sports app my heart was in my mouth, then my heart sank – 'Middlesbrough 1-0 Leeds'. I was gutted, for about three seconds, until something miraculous popped up – 'GOAL: Phillips, 90+10'. I couldn't believe my eyes; two miracles in two days! I quickly clicked on to the commentary screen, which told me it was now full time, and Leeds had rescued a point by the skin of their teeth.

Too excited to continue the journey, we popped into the services so Frankie could have a coffee and I could catch up on the story of the match in peace. The ten minutes of injury time were due to Jack Clarke falling ill during the second half. He had been taken to hospital and was recovering well, but would be unavailable for several weeks. It was another cruel and unconventional blow to the squad.

Despite dropping more points, this draw felt like a win. Keeping Middlesbrough at arm's length was important, and with two home games to come it was a result that could be built on. Leeds desperately needed to take maximum points to get their season back on track.

Leeds United 2-1 Swansea City

The Spygate saga was finally laid to rest ahead of this game, with the Football League fining the club £200,000. Leeds accepted the fine 'despite not agreeing with it', and rejected an invitation to file a complaint against the clubs who had called for a points deduction, preferring to draw a line under it and let sleeping dogs lie. Marcelo Bielsa insisted upon paying the full fine out of his own pocket, because that's the kind of man he is. Spygate may have been put to bed but the Dan James fiasco was still fresh in our minds, and Swansea made the midweek trip to Elland Road with James in their squad, contrary to the rumours he wouldn't play. The man responsible for James not being in Leeds's squad would not be present as Huw Jenkins had been sacked by Swansea's owners in the days after his act of rebellion, somehow making the whole sorry affair even more annoying.

Patrick Bamford was finally making his full league debut, and the £7m man led the line superbly as a fired-up Leeds attacked from the off. They took a deserved lead through birthday boy Pontus Jansson, and the second goal followed soon after, Jack Harrison heading home a pinpoint cross from Alioski. After a long run in the team Bielsa's faith in Harrison was starting to bear fruit as the young loanee was improving each week and this goal was a direct product of an unlikely new partnership with Gjanni Alioski. The Macedonian had been in at left-back for a few weeks in the absence of Barry Douglas, and playing his best football since signing for Leeds 18 months ago. As a winger Alioski frustrated more than he threatened, but converted to full-back he was a revelation, and so energetic it was like playing with a left-back and two left-wingers.

With a 2-0 half-time lead Leeds were primed for their first comfortable victory since August, but at 2-0 you are always acutely aware of the importance of the next goal and, despite continued domination, they couldn't kill the game off. One of the big positives of the night was the return to form of Luke Ayling. The marauding right-back had struggled since returning from injury but tonight he was back to his best. He kept Dan James under lock and key in another fruitless trip to Elland Road for the young winger, though at least he was put out of his misery early this time and was substituted midway through the second half. But Ayling's morale-boosting work unravelled when he gifted Swansea an 85th-minute lifeline. His clumsy and needless lunge resulted in a penalty, which McBurnie converted to set up another excruciating end to the match.

By now Leeds were well trained in hanging on for dear life, and Jansson and Cooper stood up to the challenge once more. The final whistle brought the biggest cheer of the night, and the second-biggest cheer soon followed; Preston had beaten Norwich 3-1 and Leeds were back on top of the league!

Leeds United 2-1 Bolton Wanderers

Thanks to their early exit from the FA Cup, Leeds enjoyed a much-needed ten-day break following the Swansea victory. The players and staff had barely had a day off all season, but El Loco granted four days for everyone to recharge their batteries and get ready for a crucial period, with six games crammed in to the next three weeks. Bielsa took advantage of the break too, and finally he was able to explore the beauty of Yorkshire. He had recently moved from the lavish Rudding Park Hotel to a modest bedsit in Wetherby from which he could walk to the training ground, and this 30-minute walk was all he had seen of Yorkshire in seven months of living here. Over the weekend photos popped up on social media of The Great Man posing for selfies with fans in various parts of our pleasant pastures. It was lovely to see.

The resting period couldn't prevent the perpetual injury curse claiming another soul, top scorer Kemar Roofe becoming the latest victim, injured when screwing wide the chance to put the Swansea game to bed. Roofe would be missing for several weeks, but with Bamford back to full fitness and Roofe suffering a goal drought, I wondered whether this would turn into a blessing in disguise, like many of the injuries had. Forshaw's pre-season injury enabled Klich to stake his claim, Pontus's early-season absence enabled Berardi to hone his skills at centre-back, Ayling's injury enabled Dallas to impress at full-back, Dallas's injury enabled Shackleton to announce himself, and Douglas's injury opened the door for Alioski to become a revelation at left-back. It was the work of a master of his trade; Bielsa doesn't squeeze square pegs into round holes, he changes the shape of the pegs.

Bolton were really struggling. Their players weren't being paid and winding-up orders seemed to come more readily than victories, so anything less than three points today would be disastrous. The match was not a classic, by any stretch of the imagination, but it had one memorable feature – Leeds were awarded a penalty! Two penalties in one season, what a time to be alive! Bamford and Hernández argued over who would take it, and Roberts was sniffing around too, but Bamford refused to relinquish the ball and confidently dispatched it into the net. You could have been forgiven for thinking today would finally be the day that the floodgates opened, but it was not to be as Bolton equalised just a few minutes later. At least Leeds had managed to avoid the dreaded 1-0 half-time lead.

The second half was as unmemorable as the first, but the goal that won the game was memorable for its comedy value, so typical of a team on their way to relegation that Bolton could have drawn a line under their season there and then. Alioski's cross took a wicked deflection, looping the ball high into the air and down towards the crossbar. As the keeper back-pedalled he fell over his own feet, flapping desperately at the ball as both fell delightfully into the goal. We still had to endure yet another nerve-wracking finale, always worse for us Kopites, trying to make sense of what is happening as high balls fly into the South Stand goalmouth, each one seeming a certain goal. Kiko and his defence stood up to the challenge once again, and by hook or by crook Leeds had claimed six points out of six, breathing life back into their season.

Our Saturday evenings have always been shaped somewhat by the result of the Leeds game, but now that we were getting to the business end of a promotion race my emotions were far more intense than Frankie had ever known. I would either come home delirious or dismayed. After a defeat I don't look at my phone or watch any football, I just try to immerse myself in whatever we are doing, even if that's just sitting at home watching *Strictly Come Dancing*. After a win it's the other end of the scale, I am insatiable for football! If free to do so, as I was after the Bolton game, I watch all the reaction on Sky Sports News while scrolling through Twitter, reading about the match and watching fans footage. Then I watch *EFL on Quest*, all the matches, through all the divisions, then it's time for *Match of the Day*, and then to bed, to scroll through Twitter one more time before lying awake, analysing the match and the permutations of the fixtures to come. Poor Frankie!

Queens Park Rangers 1-0 Leeds United

A midweek trip to Loftus Road presented Leeds with the perfect opportunity to return to the top of the table, with the home side on a run of seven straight league defeats and plummeting towards the relegation zone. Yet I was absolutely certain of a defeat. I assumed that QPR's bad run had to end, that they would be galvanised by playing Leeds and lady luck would be on their side. Sadly I wasn't wrong.

Before the game my dad questioned where the high press from earlier in the season had gone. Well if it had gone anywhere it was back now. The tempo was as intense as we'd seen for a number of weeks, probably since the Derby game, and Leeds were popping the ball around nicely too. The problem, as always, was inefficiency. Time and again Leeds got into dangerous situations, but time and again they crumbled in the final third. Then Liam Cooper picked up a nasty cut on his head, forcing him off for the last seven minutes of the first half while the medical staff stitched him up. It was a cruel blow at a crucial time in the match, and QPR's resistance may well have cracked if Cooper's head hadn't cracked first.

The second half started with QPR on the front foot and, following good work from the inspired Luke Freeman, they opened the scoring with their first shot on goal. Typical. Urged on by the rip-roaring away end, Leeds pushed for the equaliser, and chances grew in quantity and quality as the match progressed. Barry Douglas blasted a glorious chance high into the upper tier, but the worst miss was yet to come. A beautiful move started by Stuart Dallas ended with him going clear in the box, but his tame shot struck the legs of the diving keeper and the ball popped up straight on to the head of Patrick Bamford. With the goalkeeper helplessly sprawled on the floor, all Bamford needed to do was nod the ball into the empty net, but he instinctively headed it downwards, against the hapless keeper, and QPR survived. And Leeds lost.

'Bielsa burnout' is a phrase that originated when The Great Man's Athletic Bilbao side lost two cup finals at the end of the 2011/12 season (to the greatest Barcelona team of all time, and the greatest Atletico Madrid team of all time). It gathered credibility when his Marseille team tailed off in the second half of the season having lead the league at Christmas, and with Leeds struggling for consistency the theory was on the agenda again. When the interviewer mentioned burnout in the post-match interview, El Loco scoffed before Salim could even translate the question: 'The data shows that we are covering more distance than at any other stage in the season. Like all teams we have problems, but energy is never one of them.' It was a bullish response, but later that night a photo emerged of Marcelo in his most vulnerable state, crouched in the tunnel, head drooped down, alone. Bielsa was clearly suffering. It was soul-destroying to see him so down, but at the same time uplifting to see how much he cared. He would have to pick himself and the players up quickly as on Friday night there was another huge game. West Brom were coming to Elland Road on a run of nine wins from their last ten away games, looking to turn a three-horse promotion race into four. How would Leeds respond?

March 2019

1	Norwich City	66
2	Sheffield United	64
3	**Leeds**	**64**
4	West Brom	60
5	Middlesbrough	57
6	Bristol City	56

Leeds United 4-0 West Bromwich Albion

The Great Man revealed his team in the pre-match press conference, as had become standard procedure since the Spygate fiasco, as if to reaffirm his claims that football matches are won on the pitch by players, not by analysts before a ball is kicked. It would be the same team that lost at QPR just three days earlier, which was the same team that beat Bolton just three days before that, reaffirming another of Bielsa's claims – that the players were not tired. Now it was up to the players to prove him right.

I managed to slope off from work early and headed to The Boathouse on a surprisingly mild evening. The pints flowed and before we knew it we were in danger of missing kick-off, but thankfully our taxi driver knew a shrewd shortcut, avoiding all the heavy traffic and getting us to Elland Road in no time. The Woollards went into the East Stand and Justin and I headed for the Kop, feeling smug that we'd managed to sneak in an extra pint without missing kick-off, then suddenly there was an explosion of noise that could only mean one thing – a goal for Leeds! We looked at our phones which told us it was 7.45pm. How was it possible?

We got into the ground and the scoreboard confirmed what we already knew – that we had missed the dream start. My dad filled in the blanks by telling me that Hernández had scored the goal of the season, a peach of a drive into the top corner with just 13 seconds on the clock, later confirmed as the second-fastest goal ever scored at Elland Road. Funnily enough, the fastest was also scored while I was making my way into the ground, back in 2004 vs Burnley. That game descended into the worst Leeds performance I had ever seen (though there have been many worse since), but on this occasion the early goal was followed by one of the best Leeds performances I've ever seen as they absolutely battered West Brom from start to finish.

My favourite aspect of Bielsa's football has to be the non-stop tenacity off the ball, and tonight West Brom couldn't catch their breath for white shirts crawling all over them. It was phenomenal. When checking match stats I'm always interested in the number of tackles, especially compared with passing stats of the opposition. In the Premier League the numbers are painfully low, and there have been games when Manchester City's opponents have averaged a tackle every 200 passes; tonight Leeds averaged a tackle for every eight West Brom passes. That's the type of football I love to see; combative and aggressive, played in a good, fair spirit. The Bielsa Way.

The second goal came on the half-hour when Roberts slipped in Bamford, who took a touch to set himself, held off his man, and coolly slotted the ball into the far corner. The third came on the hour as Roberts slipped in Bamford, who took a touch to set himself, held off his man, and this time beat the keeper at his near post, via a nice little deflection.

Leading 3-0, Leeds finally had the comfortable scoreline they had waited nearly all season for. The fans may have been able to relax but the players continued their incessant chasing, harrying, and pulverising of West Brom. Against his former club, Tyler Roberts had the best game of his young career, but Leeds's performance was epitomised by Gjanni Alioski. On paper he was playing at left-back, but in practice Alioski was absolutely everywhere. I've never seen anything quite like it and he was a man possessed, chasing the ball around wherever it went like a dog chasing a rabbit. With the clock ticking down Justin and I agreed that a goal for Alioski would cap the night off perfectly, and in injury time the Macedonian popped up in the six-yard box to make it 4-0, delivering full retribution for the 4-1 thrashing received from West Brom on my birthday.

As the players lined up in front of me for the strangest celebration of the season, Justin commented that I looked emotional. I really was. I was so proud that Leeds had delivered a performance that perfectly reflected Marcelo Bielsa's philosophy; the greatest performance since the Champions League quarter-final thumping of Deportivo 18 years earlier. It was truly one for the ages and Alioski's goal pushed me from overjoyed to overwhelmed, especially as I'd found out the previous day that I was going to become a dad for the first time.

Bristol City 0-1 Leeds United

Having charged up the league with a long run of victories, Bristol City were now suffering from a dip in form and a severe injury crisis. In contrast, the plague of injuries that had been such a feature of Leeds's season had kindly eased and Bielsa was able to name another unchanged team. It was a good old-fashioned Saturday 3pm kick-off, and today there was added spice from the Spygate legacy as Bristol City's chairman had been the man leading the calls for a points deduction. This is a bloke who sits on the EFL board of directors, along with the CEO of, you guessed it, Derby County!

At 2.30pm, awash with anxiety, I took my negative energy upstairs and patiently waited for the real pain to begin. I was expecting a really tough away game, but it quickly settled into the pattern of a typical home match, with Jansson and Cooper mopping up long balls with ease, and Leeds in total control of possession, camped in opposition territory. Midway through the half the full-backs combined to create the opening goal for Bamford, but it came at a price.

In applying the clever finish, Bamford had crashed into keeper and post and was really struggling to get about the pitch. Bielsa gave him until half-time to recover, but soon into the second half it was clear he couldn't continue. Without Bamford the rest of the game was a struggle. Leeds weren't able to build any sustained attacks and instead resorted to a great deal of time-wasting to repel any Bristol threat, something I'd not seen from El Loco's team before. Nowadays you would call it 'game management', and Leeds managed the game superbly, thus the three points were secured without any major panic.

That had not stopped me from majorly panicking, I hated the game. I was a bag of nerves throughout and I couldn't even celebrate Bamford's goal. When the final whistle went I took a big, deep breath, looked at myself in the wardrobe mirror, and burst out laughing. I was laughing at myself for being in such a state, but laughing too out of joy and relief. Leeds remained in second, still two points behind Norwich, and two points ahead of Sheffield United, who were winning every week and due at Elland Road in seven days' time.

Reading 0-3 Leeds United

My second away game of the season came on a mild spring evening in Berkshire. I wasn't eligible for a place in the Leeds end so joined the Reading Supporters' Club in order to buy tickets in the home end for me and George, as near to the northern monkeys as we could get. I drove down in the morning, had a quick meeting with my work colleagues in Weybridge, rushed over to Reading, checked in to my B&B, and headed to the local Brewdog to meet George. A couple of pints and a Five Guys set us up nicely, and off we went to cheer on the mighty Royals.

The mighty Royals weren't so mighty this season, but they were fresh from a mighty win at the weekend when two injury-time goals had saved them from a catastrophic defeat to Bolton and eased their relegation worries. I suspected Reading might struggle to raise their game after such an epic win, but it was hard to say whether that transpired because Leeds were so superior; a completely different class to the home team.

With Hernández pulling the strings in midfield, Reading couldn't get near the Leeds players or their penalty box, and it wasn't long before that dominance was turned into goals. A nice move released Ayling down the right and his cutback found Klich arriving late, so the Pole calmly stroked the ball into the net. It looked as easy as it sounds. Hernández doubled the lead with a lovely turn and finish on the edge of the box, before making it 3-0 with another peach into the top corner. All the while George and I sat on our hands.

Leeds continued their dominance in the second half and it was the most comfortable game of the season so far, but I still couldn't relax, not until they made it 4-0. If they had, I'd have probably needed a fifth, but Bamford missed a series of chances so the game ended in a very satisfying 3-0 win.

At the final whistle all the secret Leeds fans around us revealed themselves. There was a good busload of us and we gave a nice rendition of 'We are Leeds' before ejecting ourselves from the ground. Once back in the Brewdog for our nightcap, we saw that Sheffield United had managed to win 2-0 with only ten men, their sixth win and sixth clean sheet in a row. The gap remained at two points heading into a crunch Yorkshire derby at Elland Road. The match couldn't have been set up better, and I couldn't have timed my spring break worse.

Leeds United 0-1 Sheffield United

Back in September, Frankie and I were planning a short trip in March to use up the rest of her holiday allowance before it reset in April. For various reasons our only availability was the weekend of 16 March, when Leeds were due to play Sheffield United at a crucial stage of the season, and it was also FA Cup quarter-final weekend. It was a risk booking anything, but I was more bothered about the potential of missing the cup game (if I was to miss an important league match, at least it would mean Leeds were still in the promotion hunt, and I could handle that). With Leeds falling at the first hurdle, I needed Sheffield United to go on a great cup run, so if they reached the quarter-finals I'd be off the hook altogether. The idiots lost at home to Barnet, so it transpired that I wouldn't just be missing an important league game, I'd be missing the most important league game in almost a decade.

I woke up in my Chicago bedroom at 4.30am and spent three hours stressing about the match. Ironically, it was nearly postponed due to a waterlogged pitch, but sadly the club's heroic groundsmen saved the day. Leeds started fantastically well; Bamford had a chance, Roberts had a chance, Harrison had a chance, but the ball just wouldn't go in the net. Towards the end of the half Sheffield United weathered the storm and missed a couple of opportunities themselves, but there was no doubt that the first half belonged to Leeds. More of the same would surely deliver victory, and a five-point cushion in the all-important top two.

My stomach was in knots and my nerves were transmitting to Frankie, who was in bits herself, worried about the impact a negative result would have on the trip. I tried to convince her that I'd be fine if we lost, but my actions drowned out my words; there was no hiding how vital the next 45 minutes were. The second half started well as Hernández was dictating all of Leeds's good work and it was his clever ball to Klich that set up the defining moment of the match, and possibly the promotion race. Klich's pull-back found Tyler Roberts, who hit a sweet strike towards the top corner, past the despairing dive of the keeper, but not past the post, which deflected the ball to safety.

I imagine Elland Road had the same air of 'here we go again' as I was feeling, and midway through the second half disaster did indeed strike. With Billy Sharp on his heels, Liam Cooper made a meal of dealing with a routine clearance and was robbed by the wily old fox. Sharp fed Chris Basham, who had the freedom of Elland Road and slid the ball past Kiko Casilla to give the Blades the lead. Things took another turn for the worse when a knee injury to Pontus Jansson severely hindered our desperate push for an equaliser. It was clear he couldn't continue, but with three substitutions already made Pontus soldiered on, limping up front while Phillips covered him in defence. Moments later the big Swede had the big chance to equalise. It wasn't easy as the returning Jack Clarke's pull-back was slightly behind him and arriving at pace. It probably required the finishing instincts of a wily old fox like Sharp, not a no-nonsense limping centre-back. Pontus got a good connection with his right foot but steered the ball agonisingly wide of the near post. The scenes if that had gone in!

As the game crept into injury time Cooper made his second mistake of the season, slicing a routine clearance up in the air.

Thankfully Kalvin Phillips was covering, but with Sharp on his heels, Phillips made his second mistake of the season too, miscontrolling the high ball, and Sharp was in again. Kiko was out, miles out of his goal, and rugby-tackled Sharp to keep Leeds in the match. Kiko received his marching orders accordingly and Leeds were in complete disarray. Without a keeper or an available substitution, the injured centre-back-turned-striker was now converted into emergency goalkeeper, tasked with facing a 25-yard free kick. Amid all the chaos and impending doom, I still raised a smile when the Leeds wall turned to their keeper for instructions on where to position themselves, but Pontus didn't have a clue and just shrugged helplessly. It was no surprise then that the wall didn't do its job, but thankfully Phillips had cleverly retreated to assist Jansson and headed the goal-bound shot clear.

The game was still alive, but there were only minutes of injury time left. With the last action Leeds forced a corner, so the injured centre-back-turned-striker-turned-goalkeeper headed back up the pitch to play emergency match-saver. Not all superheroes wear capes, remember, but SuperSwede would have needed his if he was to stand a chance of meeting this corner, which was woefully overhit and sailed straight out of play. With that, the match was over. Leeds had lost, and Sheffield United took control of the promotion race.

This was a hard one to take. It was St Patrick's Day, a huge event in Chicago, when they dye the river green and the streets are littered with drunk Americans partying from morning to night. A chance to drink away the pain? With Frankie pregnant it wasn't really an option. I spent the day pretending not to feel sick as a parrot, but ironically picked up food poisoning later in the day. At least I didn't have to continue the charade any longer, I was sick as a parrot for the rest of the trip. To twist the knife a little further, it was now time for the last international break of the season, and on the other side of the break Millwall were waiting again.

Leeds United 3-2 Millwall

A fortnight spent mulling over the Sheffield United result was no good for the mind or soul. Leeds may have proved they were the better of the two teams, but would that even matter at this stage of the season? It was now a question of who could hold their nerve. There had been lots of premature talk of run-ins, cup finals, and destiny in or out of Leeds's hands, but now there could be no denying we were on the home straight of the season as eight games over the next five weeks would decide the club's fate: Premier League, or the play-offs.

The mental anguish notwithstanding, an international break proved helpful in affording Pontus the time to recover from his knee injury, so his name in the line-up was a lovely surprise. There was also a surprise in the stands. My nephew had been bitten by the bug after taking my seat for the Sheffield United game and was now desperate to go every week, so my dad made the ultimate sacrifice and gave up his ticket for today's game so Lucca could go. What a grandfather! He still drove us to the game too, mainly for his fish and chips, but also to see if he could pick up a ticket outside. Amazingly he did get one, at face value in the Scratching Shed, where it all started for him 60 years ago.

The sun was shining and the atmosphere was white-hot, but the Leeds defence was caught cold as Millwall opened the scoring within minutes of the kick-off. This would be a real test of character for the players, and a test of faith for the Elland Road faithful. The crowd failed their test miserably and soon the nervous energy of the terraces transferred to the pitch as the players started to make mistakes and the crowd's agitation grew; a vicious cycle. But then came a lifeline as

Alioski was sent tumbling in the box and the referee pointed at the penalty spot. What a relief! The crowd held their breath, but Bamford fluffed his lines and his feeble effort down the middle was saved by the keeper's legs. We were still shaking our heads in disbelief when the players atoned in terrific fashion. Cooper dispossessed a Millwall attacker by the corner flag in front of me, starting a move that flowed diagonally up the pitch and ended with Pablo Hernández steering a lovely finish into the far corner. It took less than 20 seconds to get the ball from the byline into the Millwall net, and surely it was one of the goals of the season. Footage would later be released of an almost identical goal scored by El Loco's Chile team almost a decade earlier; it was vintage Bielsaball.

In the second half Leeds really hit their stride and I felt strangely calm and confident. Faith! I had faith, I knew they would win if the pressure was maintained. But the push for the winner left Leeds vulnerable at the back, and out of nothing Millwall somehow had three men over on a counterattack. Cooper managed to get back, but his desperate lunge took man instead of ball, giving away a stonewall penalty that was tucked away with ease. The Millwall players predictably taunted the South Stand instead of celebrating with their own fans just a few yards away. News then filtered through that Sheffield United were winning 2-1 and promotion was slipping away, so Leeds simply had to turn this game around.

Barry Douglas was Bielsa's first signing, he had been voted the Championship's best left-back the previous season, and was regarded a real coup at £3m. However, injuries had blighted his season and with half an hour to go he picked up another. Leeds had again used all their subs, so the Scot brave-heartedly soldiered on, playing the remainder of the match with a season-ending injury, and setting up the equaliser with a perfect cross for Luke Ayling to power into the roof of the net. Elland Road exploded with a wall of noise like I hadn't heard for many years and the 'WE ARE LEEDS' that followed the goal was deafening. It took me back to the Bristol Rovers match in 2010 when, with their team down to ten men, the Leeds fans played as the 11th man as well as the 12th, sucking the ball into the net twice to turn the game around and secure automatic promotion. 'They've just crumbled, Bristol Rovers. The sheer volume of noise from the Leeds fans has terrified them!' Charlie Nicholas's report on *Soccer Saturday* will never fail to give me goosebumps.

Leeds again pushed for the winner and everything was going through Pablo Hernández who seemed hell-bent on winning the match all by himself, though sometimes he did let his friends play too. As the game entered its final stages Hernández started another attack, sharing the ball with Roberts out on the left, where he headed for the byline and drilled in a low cross that evaded the keeper and defence. Arriving in the box was who else but Pablo Hernández, diverting the ball into an open goal and sending Elland Road delirious. I was shaking Lucca, and the bloke next to me accidentally punched me in the face, but I didn't care enough to even acknowledge his apology let alone accept it. I was in overdrive, swept by a wave of emotion that I couldn't control or describe. Leeds had saved their season, and I'm slightly embarrassed to admit that being against Millwall made the emotion even more intense; good was going to overcome evil after all!

Then suddenly my dad appeared behind us. Was I in some strange dream?! He had made his way round to the Kop once the gates were opened but had missed the winning goal in the process. The final whistle blew and the jubilant celebrations resumed, with the jubilation rising another notch when the final scores appeared on the big screen. Sheffield United 2-3 Bristol City! Bristol had scored two goals almost simultaneously with the turnaround at Elland Road, and Leeds were back in the top two!

What an incredible afternoon it had been; my favourite match for many years, so good that it inspired me to start documenting this extraordinary season from the beginning. My son would need to know the story in all its glory, however it ended. As we headed back up Beeston Hill it occurred to me that we might not have to play Millwall again next season, a thought that made me happier still. Normally in football you look forward to playing the teams you hate, but Millwall are different. I hoped I'd never see them at Elland Road again.

The Run-In

1	Norwich City	81
2	**Leeds**	**76**
3	Sheffield United	74
4	West Brom	70
5	Bristol City	64
6	Aston Villa	60

Birmingham City 1-0 Leeds United

As well as the weight of expectation, history, and desperation that the players carry on their shoulders each week, they also have to face opponents who are galvanised simply by playing against Leeds United. Maybe not so much at Elland Road, which could now be classed as a fortress again, but certainly at away games, where opponents play in the best atmosphere they've had all season and normally in front of huge TV audiences, with the chance to scupper Bielsa's promotion push now adding a further edge. I sincerely doubt that players or fans are excited by the prospect of playing Norwich or Sheffield United, it's simply a game they expect to lose. My theory that teams are more motivated against Leeds than their rivals would face the litmus test over the next few days, with the fixture list producing an unlikely scenario as Leeds's next two games were identical to Sheffield United's: Birmingham away, and Preston away.

Birmingham had recently been docked nine points for breaching EFL profit and sustainability regulations and were sliding dangerously towards the relegation zone, on a run of five straight defeats, with star striker Che Adams on an eight-match goal drought. These factors scared the life out of me and I was all too aware that the Football Gods love turning the tables when Leeds are involved.

On a bright day at St Andrew's, Leeds made a bright start. Birmingham were allowing them all the possession they wanted, happy to defend their own half and hoping to feast on scraps at the other end. We'd seen these tactics work for Garry Monk at Elland Road (for and against Leeds), but even so, I was more than happy with the first half-hour. Then in the 30th minute came a pivotal moment in the promotion race as Luke Ayling's cross found Bamford, eight yards out and all alone, with the goalkeeper in no-man's-land having misjudged the cross. The ball was at an awkward height, but header or volley, this was surely a certain goal. Not so, as Bamford's left-footed prod bounced the ball against the inside of the post and into the grateful arms of the observing goalkeeper. Seconds later the ball was in the Leeds net, who else but Che Adams with a powerful finish from the edge of the box, and seconds after that Sheffield United took the lead at Preston.

In the second half Leeds's performance tailed off alarmingly, and even Pablo, scintillating in recent weeks, was having a stinker. Kiko Casilla was the only player to do himself justice, making a hat-trick of saves to keep Leeds alive, but his heroics only brought a slower and more painful death. Patrick Bamford completed a 'perfect hat-trick' of his own, adding to his left-footed sitter in the first half by firing right-footed high over the bar from eight yards, and heading straight at the keeper from six yards. There were six added minutes at the end of the 90, but by this point Leeds weren't even threatening to threaten, and I was so forlorn that the final whistle almost came as a relief. Birmingham's five-game losing run was over, Adams's drought was over, and with Sheffield United claiming victory at Preston it felt like the world was over. Leeds were down to third again.

Typically, Bielsa blamed himself for the defeat, as apparently he'd got Klich's positioning wrong in the first half and chose the wrong options from the bench in the second half. The Great Man's explanations may have been valid, but I couldn't agree with the blanket acceptance of blame. The players had been dreadful in that second half, their worst performance of the season.

Preston North End 0-2 Leeds United

It took me three days to get over the Birmingham defeat, and in that time I went through three of the five stages of grief; anger (at the performance), depression (over the result), and finally on Tuesday morning, acceptance (they wouldn't deserve automatic promotion if they kept slipping up). With Sheffield United playing twice before Leeds played again, defeat at Deepdale could mean a seven-point deficit by the time they kicked another ball, so it felt like win or bust tonight. Incredibly for the modern game, Leeds's outfield ten was unchanged for the ninth successive game. Hernández retained his place despite leaving Birmingham with his foot in a protective boot, and Bamford stayed in despite coming under fire from the Leeds fans. Perhaps he was still rusty from missing nearly the whole season with two separate knee injuries, but there was no time for patience; goals and performances were needed with no time to waste.

After an even first ten minutes Leeds began to stamp their authority on the match. Pablo was pulling the strings, Phillips was patrolling midfield, Ayling and Alioski were flying down the wings, but at half-time there were no goals to show for that domination. Early in the second half Leeds were given a helping hand by one of the rarest creatures found on these shores; a referee who was kind to them throughout. Although generosity played no part when Bamford was bundled over as he raced clean through on goal. The ref had no choice but to brandish his red card and reduce the hosts to ten men. As the clock ticked past the hour mark Leeds were probing but anxiety was rising, then the ball fell to BAAAAMFOOORD! A magnificent goal out of nowhere, a 25-yard thunderbolt that flew into the corner, sending the 5,500 Leeds fans wild. The dominance continued but with a calmer, more patient approach, and Leeds put the game to bed when Klich crossed for Bamford to plant a beautiful header into the top corner. Wham, bam, thank you, Patrick!

Despite trailing Sheff United's goal difference by four goals, Leeds were content to see out the game safely. We weren't to know whether Leeds would regret not scoring more goals on nights like these, but I knew one person who had huge regrets. Kinky Dave was on for a £500 windfall if Bamford scored a hat-trick, and in the last minute he was sent clean through on goal. Bamford dillied and dallied, then dallied and dillied, and lost the chance without getting a shot away. He was then substituted immediately. Poor Kinks! But Leeds had a huge three points on the board, a victory that turned fear into hope, and now the pattern of fixtures looked in their favour. With Sheffield United playing twice in a row, if they didn't win both games then destiny would be back in Leeds's hands.

The next evening Sheffield United were held to an ugly 1-1 draw by Birmingham, and with Norwich's eight-match winning run finally coming to an end I found myself analysing their (pretty tough) run-in, and dreaming about the title. What a difference a day makes! Leeds would have the chance to go within three points of Norwich on Saturday evening, but far more important was the one-point lead over the Blades. Just five matches remained, with three at home, starting with the last Yorkshire derby of the season.

Leeds United 1-0 Sheffield Wednesday

The fixture list had thrown up another quirk and Sheffield United would find themselves cheering on arch-rivals Wednesday in the Saturday evening kick-off at Elland Road, with Leeds cheering on Millwall, of all teams, in the 3pm kick-off at Bramall Lane. The prospect of arriving at Elland Road after a Sheffield United slip-up was truly mouth-watering; nevertheless, I was perturbed by Sky's scheduling, which had Leeds playing after the Blades in every round of matches until the last day of the season. I didn't know whether this would help or hinder but it certainly seemed unethical, and I would have thought the EFL could have blocked such a proposal on sporting grounds. Whether ignorant to the inequality, conniving against Leeds, or slaves to the money, it didn't sit well.

A lovely morning stroll in the Yorkshire Dales with Frankie did nothing to quell my anxiety, so once my husband duties were complete I jumped on the next train to Leeds to meet the Woollards, with pre-match nerve-settlers deemed more important than fish and chips today (forgive me, father, for I have sinned). We tracked the Sheffield United game over a few pints in The Boathouse, then jumped in a taxi to Elland Road with the Blades 1-0 up in the closing stages. To my dismay, the driver reported that Millwall had just missed a penalty, awarded after the defender had punched the ball off the goal line to prevent a certain goal. I couldn't believe our luck. While we queued for one last pint at The Peacock I was frantically checking my phone for a miracle equaliser, but my 3G was struggling in the big crowd. The bloke next to me had no such problems and showed me his phone; 94th minute, still 1-0. 'It's over,' he said. Just then, from the back of the beer garden cheers swept towards me like a tsunami. It could only mean one thing, Millwall had equalised! Everyone was celebrating in disbelief, and out of nowhere Leeds had the chance to take control of the promotion race and the opportunity to move three points clear. I couldn't believe the stroke of luck!

There was still time for more pre-match drama as Liam Cooper was injured in the warm-up, meaning a first start in six months for cult hero Gaetano Berardi. Bera had refused an operation at Christmas that would have ruled him out for the season, as he'd wanted to do everything he could to be available, if and when called upon, to help the team to promotion. The time was now.

For the first time this season Leeds were forced to attack the Kop in the first half, but considering the amount of half-time leads they'd had I saw this as a blessing in disguise, and maybe they could blow Wednesday away. They did just that, but still there was no half-time lead. Back in 2008, goalkeeper Kieran Westwood had the game of his life playing for Carlisle United in the League One play-offs at Elland Road, keeping Leeds at bay during a first-half onslaught at the Kop end. Eleven years later we saw a repeat performance, Westwood making the save of the season from a point-blank Roberts header, before denying Harrison with another miraculous stop.

In the second half the Leeds fans stepped up to the plate, and the atmosphere was electric. 'We are the champions, champions of Europe' echoed around the ground perpetually, scarves spinning everywhere you looked, and we were doing all we could to drag the team over the line. Pontus powered a free header inches over the bar, Bamford screwed a golden chance wide from six yards, and still the fans kept spurring

Leeds on – 'We are the champions, champions of Europe' – and after 20 minutes of incessant chanting we were rewarded with the breakthrough. Pablo found space on the right of the box and played a trademark pass through the defender's legs to Harrison, whose deft finish squeezed through another defender's legs, through the tiny gap between the grasping fingers of Westwood and the far post, and into the net. The celebrations were so wild that one lad was carried out of the South Stand with a broken ankle, although he didn't seem to care one jot.

With the season's finish line ever closer, the atmosphere changed and the cauldron of noise became a cauldron of nerves, but on the pitch Leeds remained in full control. The players were now dragging the fans through the game. Only in the very last minute did Wednesday threaten when a goalbound strike was crucially blocked by none other than Berardi, and the rebound was smashed into the side netting. Huge sighs of relief were soon followed by huge cheers as the final whistle blew and Leeds were closing in on the Promised Land; three points clear with four games to play.

In midweek fear had turned to hope, but now hope had turned to belief. Coming next was the Easter weekend, a double-header of fixtures that could see Leeds promoted on Easter Monday, if Sheffield United failed to get a win from two tricky games against Forest and Hull. 'The gap is not big enough,' said Bielsa, who wasn't urging caution. He was just telling a simple truth, the gap wasn't big enough. Leeds were close, but one defeat would snatch destiny from their hands again.

Leeds United 1-2 Wigan Athletic

Good Friday, and it felt like the first day of summer, with blazing sunshine and not a cloud in the sky. My dad and Lucca picked me up and we listened to Sheffield United v Forest on the journey to Elland Road. I was hopeful that Forest could get something, and if they did Leeds were almost there, but the radio let me down once again as the Blades ground out a 2-0 victory. Leeds had dropped to third, but the live table would shunt them back into second as soon as they kicked off against lowly Wigan.

In the chippy there was good news and bad news; two fish for me, the first double-up of the season, but Liam Cooper had failed a late fitness test. An unchanged team didn't cause any great alarm, though, as today's opponents were deep in the relegation dogfight and hadn't won away from home all season. As we walked down Beeston Hill we noticed a plane flying over Elland Road displaying the message 'BIELSA IS GOD'. We gawped blissfully, heedless of God's abysmal record on Good Friday.

Leeds were turned around for the second game running and barely touched the ball for the first ten minutes, but when they finally launched their first attack it ended in a penalty and a red card to Wigan's centre-back. Replays showed it to be a terrible decision, and some justice was done as Pablo Hernández smacked the penalty against the post. The Kop bellowed out the Spaniard's name as if the penalty had gone in, and just a few minutes later the miss was rendered irrelevant as Bamford rifled home a superb opening goal. It had already been a carnival atmosphere and now it was party time. With a 1-0 lead against ten men, ten of the worst men in the league, the cat was in the bag. The knot just needed to be tied. Leeds went searching for the second goal, to finish the game and open the floodgates, but despite acres of space down each wing they just weren't clicking and struggled to create any clear chances. As time wore on the party died down, and in the 44th minute disaster struck when ten-man Wigan breached the defence and smashed home the equaliser. The party was over and Elland Road was shell-shocked.

I had been agitated throughout the first half, and through the half-time break my agitation turned to panic, yet deep down we all expected the winning goal would come. It duly came on the hour, but to the disbelief of everyone inside Elland Road it was ten-man Wigan who got it. A long ball was pumped into the box, Wigan won both headers, and the ball was in the net. Having fretted about the prospect of dropping two points, Leeds were now in grave danger of not even getting the one point needed to keep their destiny in their own hands. The nervous tension in the ground was palpable as relentless attacks broke down time and time again. Leeds racked up 36 shots, 59 crosses, and nearly 80 per cent possession, but it was Wigan who came closest to scoring again, striking the bar from a free kick. The final whistle blew and the Leeds players collapsed on the pitch; defeat had been clawed from the jaws of victory, the most inconceivable defeat I have ever witnessed.

Eventually the crestfallen whites took their customary lap of honour, the fans honoured them by singing their support, but it felt like relegation. I don't know why, but I couldn't bring myself to leave the stadium; a feeling that was shared by Pablo, Pontus, and Alioski, who stood motionless in the centre circle long after the final whistle, gazing on in disbelief, staring into the abyss.

Once home, I went straight to bed. I just wanted to go to sleep and wake up on Monday for the next match, Brentford away, another game I was certain would be lost. Bielsa's post-match words were ringing around my head: 'The only way we can fix the pain of this defeat is to get promoted.' Never a truer word spoken, I bloody love that man. As I lay in bed I daydreamed of turning back the clock. Back to before the game when Leeds were on the brink of promotion. If Forest didn't get that dodgy red card it could all have been different. Back to the first half when Leeds were 1-0 up, how did they not score again? How did they let ten-man Wigan clean through on goal? Back to half-time, the whole second half to come, did Leeds really need to make a double substitution? Back to injury time, just to have that measly five minutes again, how could they not somehow force the equaliser?

Leeds had threatened to batter someone all season and this match should have finished 5-0. Even the Wigan manager admitted he just wanted to keep the score down after Bamford's opener. Instead Leeds had committed suicide. The players played like I'd felt; too desperate for the second goal, so desperate they forgot how to play. In less of a pressure-cooker atmosphere they would have passed the ball calmly around defence, slowly grinding Wigan down, but the three points were so close they took a running jump for them and fell flat on their faces. Suddenly the season was in tatters and from the brink of promotion Leeds were now on the brink of the play-offs. I had no idea how they could recover physically and mentally in time to win at Brentford on Easter Monday, where, almost comically, they hadn't won since 1950.

Brentford 2-0 Leeds United

It had taken a couple of days, but I was once again at peace with the world after the shock of the worst Good Friday in 2,019 years. I was still dreaming of another twist in the promotion race, but I didn't believe. It was another glorious sunny day and a good crew of us arranged to meet at The Alex to track the Sheffield United game at 3pm. I was the first to arrive, and by the time Ads joined me the Blades were already 2-0 up, and by half-time it was 3-0, from three shots at goal. From all accounts, Hull played like they were already on the beach. 'Maybe we'll get the same courtesy from Brentford?' I sarcastically wondered.

In the knowledge that defeat at Griffin Park would all but end their automatic promotion bid, Leeds started with the bit between their teeth. Bamford missed a decent chance, Roberts inexplicably overran the ball when clean through, but even more inexplicable was the referee's decision to wave away a stonewall penalty when Bamford was tripped right in front of him. Soon Brentford worked their way into the game, and before half-time Neal Maupay capitalised on another gaping hole in Leeds's defence and calmly beat Casilla. The players never looked like recovering. Clarke came on for the second half but couldn't do anything right, nobody could, and Brentford soon scored again to move out of sight. At the final whistle the players were heartbroken as they knew it was as good as over, and in a rare personal touch Bielsa walked around the Griffin Park pitch consoling every one of them.

Although I was very sad (Pablo Hernández in tears was an especially soul-destroying image), I had been mentally prepared. I knew 'ten-man Wigan' was terminal for the promotion bid. I was feeling philosophical enough to chew the fat on the phone to Lewis while I walked home. We discussed our long list of regrets; the loss of Sáiz, the distraction of Spygate, missing out on Dan James, Jack Clarke's illness, the defeat to Sheffield United, all those bloody injuries. In the end, though, we agreed that Leeds simply weren't good enough in the final third. Scoring goals is the hardest thing in football and they couldn't do it as efficiently as Sheffield United and Norwich.

The last glimmer of hope now lay with rock-bottom, already relegated, Ipswich Town. If they got a result at Bramall Lane, and Leeds could beat Aston Villa (who were on a ten-match winning run), the promotion race would go to the last day. However, the chances of another team managing to 'do a Leeds' seemed almost impossible.

Leeds United 1-1 Aston Villa

And so it came to pass; no team is capable of doing a Leeds, except Leeds. On Saturday evening Sheffield United swept Ipswich aside with ease while I watched the snooker (I couldn't bear to watch the promotion party that should have been ours). Norwich were now the best hope as their goal difference was only better than Leeds's by ten, but two hours later they beat Blackburn 2-1 to secure the Championship title. The promotion bid was still not mathematically over, but a 13-goal swing was never going to happen, so all that remained was to dot the i's and cross the t's. However, in 2018/19 nothing would pass quietly. Even a dead rubber turned into an unforgettable afternoon at Elland Road.

The last home game of the league campaign was a high-noon showdown between the two biggest clubs in the division – two of the biggest clubs in the country. There was a defiant atmosphere at Elland Road, albeit with a hint of sorrow. Until last week, everyone in attendance had expected this match to be the crowning glory of Leeds's promotion season, and as the players emerged from the tunnel it was impossible not to daydream of a different scenario. The star of the first half was referee Stuart Attwell, with Villa's talisman Jack Grealish acting as his sidekick. Grealish was a highly rated talent who played a version of the game that was closer to American football. On receiving the ball, he would drive forward until a Leeds player came close enough for him to throw himself to the floor, or sometimes he would even just turn to Attwell and throw his hands in the air. Attwell would award the free kick and Villa would have gained a few yards. This tactic stifled Leeds's aggressive pressing game and infuriated the crowd, bringing the atmosphere to boiling point.

Fury gave way to fun when, after another 'foul' on Grealish, Attwell trotted over to the Leeds bench and booked Bielsa! The Leeds fans were dumbfounded, and on his 100-yard journey back over to the north-east corner – where Villa were waiting to take the free kick – Attwell received the most sarcastic standing ovation you could ever witness; the whole of Elland Road was on their feet, cheering and clapping until the free kick was taken. By the end of the half we were furious again, with Attwell blowing for half-time just as Luke Ayling broke through the Villa defence. In a match that was practically meaningless, the referee had the Leeds players and fans all baying for blood.

In the second half the spotlight was well and truly taken away from Attwell as one of the biggest stories of the English football season developed (arguably only second only to Spygate). It all started when a Leeds player went down injured during a Villa attack, and after some persuasion – once any danger had passed – Villa sportingly put the ball out of play. A few minutes later, Villa's Jonathan Kodjia went down injured in the middle of the Leeds half, then five slick passes later and Tyler Roberts had the ball on the left wing. The Villa players were waving their hands in the air, asking for the game to be stopped, and for a moment Roberts looked like he was going to obey them, but instead he passed the ball and the responsibility on to Mateusz Klich. The Pole was having none of it and headed straight for goal, cut inside and swerved a lovely finish low into the far corner. It may have been a meaningless goal, but the Leeds fans went potty. I celebrated like promotion was still on the line, thrilled that Villa had their comeuppance for all the play-acting. The Villa players were incensed and a 22-man melee broke out. The Kop were absolutely loving it: 'If you hate Leeds United, hate Leeds United, hate Leeds United have a go!' A smoke bomb went off to add to the drama, and when the yellow smoke cleared I noticed the retractable tunnel was out, so someone must have been sent off. A quick count of the players and Villa were down to ten. Great!

What I hadn't noticed was Bielsa on the touchline screaming at his players to let Villa score. 'GIVE THE GOAL, GIVE THE GOAL!' Villa kicked off, and to everybody's bewilderment the Leeds players stood and watched as Albert Adomah headed towards goal. Pontus Jansson was the only Judas among the disciples and made a half-hearted lunge for the ball, but Adomah rode the challenge and scored into the unguarded net. 'What the fuck is going on?' asked the gobsmacked Leeds fans. Although I respected El Loco's decision, it was one that I disagreed with, only due to the conduct of the Villa players before, during, and after the incident. We had played to the whistle, while they had tried to gain advantages at every turn.

Roared on by the electrified crowd, Leeds piled forward, but despite the extra man, the chances, and the goalmouth scrambles, they just couldn't force the winner. The promotion race was officially over, and Bielsa had given away the goal that condemned his side to the dreaded play-offs. Nevertheless, Elland Road was in fine spirits during the end-of-season lap of honour and this was just what we had needed – a defibrillator to restart our hearts and renew our hope.

Ipswich Town 3-2 Leeds United

In the aftermath of the Villa game The Great Man received plaudits from all over the world for his actions, though back home Leeds still came out of it looking like the bad guys. Patrick Bamford received a two-match ban for simulation,

Villa's Anwar El Ghazi had his red card rescinded, and Conor Hourihane, who was caught on camera punching Klich in the stomach, 'had no case to answer'. Because Klich hadn't fallen to the floor, the EFL's three-man panel decided that the punch wasn't forceful enough to warrant a ban. In his pre-match press conference, Bielsa rightly pointed out that by not banning Hourihane the EFL were encouraging the simulation they were trying to stop by banning Bamford. Bielsa also drew a line under the 'given goal' incident, explaining that his Leeds team would never again stop playing with an opponent down injured, and he expected the same behaviour from the other teams. Only the referee would decide to stop the game, as stated in the rules.

The regular season ended with the long trip to Portman Road to face an Ipswich side who were well adrift at the bottom of the league, with only four wins all season and no goals in over 300 minutes. Thanks to Bielsa's generosity, Leeds still needed a point to secure third place in the league. West Brom were two points behind them and faced Derby, who were vying with Middlesbrough for the last play-off spot. Having failed to get tickets in the Leeds end, Lewis pulled out all the stops and managed to get us tickets in the home end through a friend of a friend. This was before the unthinkable had happened, of course, so Lewis cancelled his trip from Canada and Justin accompanied me to Suffolk instead. Heading into this game, Leeds boasted an outrageously poor shot conversion rate of 2.4 per cent over the last five games (less than a goal every 40 shots), and more shoddy finishing was punished midway through the first half when more shoddy set-piece defending brought an end to Ipswich's goal drought. The ever-present Mateusz Klich equalised with his tenth goal of a great season, so at the break Leeds remained in third, and were set to face Derby in the play-offs.

The second half was an open and entertaining affair. Jason Dozzell's son, Andre, put Ipswich 2-1 up, Pablo missed an open goal after good work from Jack Clarke – the first good work he had contributed since being taken ill at Middlesbrough – and a lovely move finally brought the second equaliser with 15 minutes to go. In the closing stages Leeds were awarded yet another penalty, bringing yet another red card for their opponents, and with three points seemingly in the bag, yet another spectacular capitulation. Kemar Roofe became the third player in five weeks to miss a penalty, scuffing his shot onto his ankle, which looped the ball over the bar, and the calamity was completed in injury time when Kiko and Ayling left a harmless ball to each other, allowing Ipswich's striker to tap into an empty net. It wasn't dissimilar to the Villa equaliser. The OAP next to me found it hilarious, laughing his head off and nudging me with glee: 'Hahaha, I can't believe this lot nearly got promoted, they're bloody useless! Losing to us! Hahahaha!'

After the match Bielsa tried to sweep the result under the carpet, and he was right to do so, but the manner of the defeat was another slap in the face for the fans. It had been a catastrophic end to the season. With ten points required from the last four games to seal promotion, only one had been taken. With West Brom losing to Derby, Leeds finished third despite the defeat, and Derby edged out Boro for sixth. The play-off semi-final would be a Spygate-fest for the media.

The Dreaded Play-Offs

Derby County 0-1 Leeds United

In the week leading up to the play-offs, two footballing miracles occurred in the Champions League semi-finals. On the Tuesday, Liverpool overturned a 3-0 first-leg deficit, beating Lionel Messi's Barcelona 4-0 on possibly the greatest night Anfield has ever seen. I was delighted that they won as my brother is a huge Liverpool fan and had flown in from Tokyo for the game. The next night, trailing 3-0 on aggregate with a quarter of the tie remaining, Spurs somehow dragged themselves back from the dead and a 96th-minute goal sent them through to the final on away goals. Again I was happy, this time for my boss, Chris, but deep down I felt utterly miserable that the only miracles Leeds ever produce are miraculous defeats. In years gone by I would have given my right arm to be in this position, but I was so downbeat about missing out on automatic promotion that I felt numbed to the prospect of the play-offs. It just felt cruel that we would have to go through it all again.

I had already predicted a 4-0 defeat for Leeds at Pride Park, then the news emerged that Pontus Jansson was injured. In his press conference Pontus said he would play in a wheelchair if needed, but reality prevailed and Berardi stepped in for the big Swede. After taking a well-earned break in the spring, the injury curse was firing on all cylinders again and Leeds were really down to the bare bones. The substitutes' bench comprised of six academy players and Izzy Brown, who was still stuck on one appearance, one touch, and one booking in a Leeds shirt.

My mates repeated the ill-fated Brentford plan by meeting at 3pm in The Alex, which was packed out like the good old days. As the pints flowed my numbness faded, and as the game developed our performance whipped me up into a frenzy. The first ten minutes were worrying and Leeds had to withstand heavy pressure as Derby flew out of the blocks, but when Adam Forshaw became the latest to succumb to injury, the introduction of young Jamie Shackleton coincided with Bielsa's team taking complete control. There were no goals, but no sign of any dented confidence or tiredness either, as they were playing superbly.

The second half was ten minutes old when the game was lit up by two pieces of magic, and the first came from the referee. Following a neat little interchange from a throw-in, Stuart Dallas was clattered as he passed the ball to Jack Harrison, who had three men around him and no one in support. But the ref showed Hernández-level vision in signalling 'advantage', and Harrison produced Hernández-level quality to curl a low ball around four defenders into the path of the onrushing Kemar Roofe. Roofe stabbed the ball first time into the corner of the net and the pub erupted, then everybody got showered with beer.

Leeds pushed for a second as Shackleton carried the ball 50 yards and put a chance on a plate for Hernández, but the Spaniard couldn't connect with his finish. Then Roofe had a big chance but his shot to the keeper's left was saveable, whereas a shot in the other direction would surely have bulged the net. Derby eventually weathered the storm and in the closing stages a through ball into the Leeds box brought the game's big talking point. Harrison and the Derby attacker chased the ball, Harrison swung for it but missed, and both players fell in a heap. The referee thought for a moment, then pointed at the spot. It looked a soft decision, bringing fervent appeals from the Leeds players, who begged the ref to go and speak with his linesman, and to my astonishment the ref complied. My optimism grew as the linesman assertively informed the referee about what he saw, and the pub erupted again as the referee overturned his decision and awarded the free kick to Leeds. What a let-off!

At the final whistle I was ecstatic. Leeds had secured a 1-0 lead going into the second leg and, considering the circumstances, this must have been the most impressive victory of the season. Ironically, Leeds now faced the scenario they could have faced had they beaten ten-man Wigan; draw the next game, then beat Aston Villa for promotion.

Leeds United 2-4 Derby County

During the post-match celebrations at Pride Park, the Leeds fans created a new chant mocking Frank Lampard, to the Oasis tune, 'Stop Crying Your Heart Out'. It went viral, and contained the line 'you'll beat us some day'. Talk about tempting fate with the return leg only three days away! Equally concerning was the discovery by some nerdy statistician that in over 30 years of Championship play-offs, no team had ever lost on aggregate having won the first leg away from home. Like the ill-fated 'top at Christmas' stat, this was just a quirk in the record books that was waiting to be broken; Ajax had lost in the same circumstances a week earlier, and even Leeds themselves had gone through in the League One play-offs having lost the first leg at home to Carlisle.

Regardless of all the above, I fully expected Leeds to get through to Wembley, and successfully convinced Lewis to fly back from Canada for tonight's match. He had initially planned to come home only if they got through the semi-final, but here we were, enjoying afternoon pints on a baking-hot Wednesday afternoon in Harrogate. Once in Leeds we met up with the rest of the lads, who had splashed out on an executive box in the South Stand, as it was the only way they could get tickets. I felt a nervous excitement, but was more excited than nervous; the season was on the line, and I couldn't wait for the match. We arrived at the ground to find nylon scarves laid on every seat. While I normally hate this type of forced fanfare, it cannot be denied that Elland Road looked magnificent as the teams came out; a sea of white in the setting evening sun and 'Marching On Together' belting out so loud that it completely drowned out the PA system. My dad commented that it was the loudest he had ever heard the stadium. 'You can sense it in your ears!' he declared. 'What else would you sense it with?!'

The match kicked off and Leeds took control. Every touch from the opponents was greeted with boos, as is custom for the very biggest games at Elland Road, a practice that builds a great pressure, released when Leeds win the ball back to great cheers. And the cheers reached fever pitch when Kalvin Phillips's deep free kick bounced through a crowded box, bounced off the post, and into the path of Stuart Dallas, who fired into the net, and bounced on his arse in front of the South Stand. With a 2-0 aggregate lead, Leeds had one foot on Wembley Way. Moments later, Klich's deflected shot hit the underside of the bar. Derby were clinging on by their fingernails so Lampard channelled his inner Bielsa by making a first-half tactical substitution, bringing on a new attacker to change the shape of his team. Immediately, a ball over the top of the Leeds defence changed the course of history.

Kiko Casilla had already rushed out of his goal twice. The first time he calmly dribbled round the striker and pinged the ball out to the wing, but the second time he caused mayhem and Derby fired over an open goal from 20 yards, and it was third time unlucky as Kiko rushed out again in the 44th minute. Had Cooper left it for Kiko the ball would have been cleared, and had Kiko left it for Cooper the ball would have been cleared, but the sight of Kiko rushing out panicked the captain, who couldn't have known the striker was a good two yards behind him. Cooper slid to clear the ball but didn't get enough on it, clattering Kiko in the process and enabling the Derby substitute to pounce on the loose ball and roll it into an empty net with his first touch of the game. It was an absolute calamity, yet another goal gifted away, and painfully close to half-time. But not close enough to prevent Kiko rushing out of his goal for a fourth time, causing mayhem again, though this time the loose ball was cleared in the nick of time. Elland Road was incredulous. When the half-time whistle blew the Leeds players trudged off in disbelief. Derby couldn't believe their luck and all the impetus was theirs now.

Half-time felt like Wigan all over again. Leading 2-1 on aggregate, Leeds's future was still in their own hands, but had they already committed suicide? With my mouth bone dry and my throat hoarse, I made a late decision to get a bottle of water for the second half. As I waited in the queue the players were already back out, and as I ordered my water the ball was already in the Leeds net as Derby had practically scored from kick-off and were now level on aggregate. Within minutes of getting back to my seat things got even worse when Liam Cooper needlessly pulled the shirt of a Derby attacker in the box and the ref awarded a penalty. It was all too much to take for one lad, who invaded the pitch from the Kop end. It took four stewards to stop him, but his anger would not be quelled and he fought and squirmed all the way out of the ground, by which time the penalty had been calmly stroked

The author and the president #ForzaLeedsCazzo

The Polished Turds: dressed like Real Madrid, playing like Barcelona

The iconic view from Beeston Hill

'Harrison scores, we're in the Loch...' (left to right: Billy, Rocco, Justin, Rick, Gianni, Gaz, Nige, Barker, Terry, Paul, Mike, Fran, George, Lewis, J. Woollard, Paddy)

El Mago, Pablo Hernandez

Fifty-eight games later, Leeds get another penalty

The miracle of the double Christmas miracle

Pontus' preposterous Potteries punishment

Dad's happy place

From overjoyed to overwhelmed

The secret away end at Reading

A brave face, but a broken heart

The Woollards

The 12-minute six-point swing

The Yorkshire Pirlo

Closing in on promotion

Watching disaster unfold

Leeds, Leeds have fallen apart, again

The greatest dead-rubber

Farewell Pontus (but not as well as us!)

More calamity at Ipswich

Lambs to the slaughter

Hope and expectation

Total desolation

into the corner to complete the comeback. It was 3-1 on the night and 3-2 to Derby on aggregate. Leeds got back on the front foot, and it didn't take long for Stuart Dallas to produce a wonderful equaliser, cutting in from the left and curling a low drive into the corner for 3-3 on aggregate and all to play for. The atmosphere was electric again, Leeds were well on top and playing superb football, but despite the Kop's best efforts to suck the ball home, the chances came and went.

And so to the last pivotal moment in the season; a battle for a loose ball in the centre circle. Berardi's tenacity won possession initially, but when his shirt was pulled he lost control of the ball and his discipline. A wild lunge on ex-Leeds man Bradley Johnson had the referee reaching for his pocket and it didn't matter what the colour was, as Bera had already been booked and Leeds were down to ten men. I really felt for Berardi as he was unlucky that the ref had missed the initial foul; nevertheless, it was a red-mist moment just when Leeds were back in the ascendancy. I also felt for Pontus Jansson, who had been left on the bench despite overcoming his injury, and stayed there even after his replacement had been sent off. In the biggest game of his Leeds career the only time Pontus got on the pitch was to scream at the defence during our 13-minute three-goal collapse.

Despite being a man down, Leeds were still going for it and our defence was struggling to cope. When Derby broke through only to be denied by the post it felt like a precursor rather than a warning, and with five minutes to go they broke through again to score what would surely be the winning goal. I've never seen opponents celebrate so euphorically; players, fans, and bench all going absolutely bonkers.

Bielsa threw on Jack Clarke and Izzy Brown to save the game (Brown making his home debut roughly 99.96 per cent into the season), and after some huffing and puffing Leeds got a stoppage-time lifeline – a free kick on the edge of the box, plus the significant bonus of a red card to the offending Derby player. Now there was real hope again as a goal here wouldn't just be a stay of execution; Leeds would be favourites again going into extra time. There was only one man you'd want to take responsibility for delivering the miracle moment, a goal that would define a generation, a goal that no Leeds fan would ever forget, but Pablo Hernández was limping heavily from the foul, so over trotted Izzy Brown instead. A Chelsea loanee who had barely kicked a ball for us all season really shouldn't have assumed the responsibility here, but the poetry of Brown saving our season appealed to me, so I held my breath and prayed for a goal. It had been 25 years since my prayers were last answered, and it'll probably be another 25 before they are answered again. Brown unleashed one of those stupid side-foot shots that only Ronaldo and Gareth Bale seem to pull off, and the ball sailed harmlessly over the bar. Under normal circumstances the Kop would have been baying for Brown's blood for such a pathetic attempt, but we were all too drained and dejected.

There would be one final surge to goal when Clarke picked the ball up by the corner flag and drove his defender into the box. Pablo was waving his arms, free for a cutback, but the youngster didn't look up and instead drilled a low cross that deflected into the air and safely into the keeper's hands. With that the final whistle blew, bringing the season to a heartbreaking, earth-shattering end. The players were inconsolable; there were no more chances, they had failed. Derby celebrated like they'd won the World Cup.

When I got home I watched the highlights on Sky Sports News, who described the match as the most thrilling play-off semi-final in history. It hadn't registered what sensational viewing it must have been for the neutral as the game had passed me by as a series of moments, and all I could do was wonder how on earth Leeds had lost. Had Kiko not rushed out of goal they would have won. Had Berardi not got sent off they would have won. Had Pontus played instead of watching us capitulate, maybe they would have won. Everything had fallen so perfectly into place this season, but still they managed to mess it up. I wondered how I'd ever get over it. This really went beyond 'typical Leeds'.

The Aftermath

THE CHAMPIONSHIP season ended with Aston Villa beating Derby in a dour play-off final at Wembley; two teams who had been outplayed by Leeds in all six fixtures against them. Promotion-winning manager Dean Smith, had visited Elland Road twice (he had been in charge of Brentford before moving to Villa) and his players had dived to win a penalty, headbutted Alioski, punched Klich, throttled Berardi, swung an elbow at Bamford, been given a 'walk-in goal', and still couldn't beat Leeds. Leeds had been 8-1 up on aggregate vs Derby before the 13-minute treble salvo that blew the season to smithereens.

Bielsa once said if footballers were robots he would never lose a match, and his methods had Leeds ranked first in a plethora of metrics; possession, tackles, shots, shots faced, and many more. But until Leeds ranked first in the only metric that matters, the final Championship table, he could not walk away. Thus, as the dust settled on the season, the club announced that Marcelo Bielsa would remain at Elland Road, despite interest from various glamorous clubs around the world. The painful ending had its antidote and we would go through it all again in 2019/20.

He may not have delivered promotion, but El Loco was universally adored by the Leeds fans, as a man and a manager. In a way, he had given us more than promotion; he had transformed the whole culture of the club, from the pitch right down to the core, hopefully for generations to come. But there could be no escaping the hard truth; promotion was the be-all and end-all. If Marcelo Bielsa couldn't get Leeds up, who could?

It was the brilliant David Peace who first dubbed Leeds as 'The Damned United', in the title of his best-selling novel. I never appreciated how fitting this name was until Googling the definition of 'damned' while writing this book – 'condemned by God to suffer eternal punishment in hell.' Yet when I look back on 2018/19 – the fantastic football, the wisdom of Bielsa, and the atmosphere inside Elland Road – it felt more like being condemned by God to suffer eternal punishment in heaven.

Championship Table 2018/19

		Pld	*W*	*D*	*L*	*F*	*A*	*Pts*
1	Norwich City (C)	46	27	13	6	93	57	94
2	Sheffield United (P)	46	26	11	9	78	41	89
3	**Leeds**	**46**	**25**	**8**	**13**	**73**	**50**	**83**
4	West Brom	46	23	11	12	87	62	80
5	Aston Villa (P)	46	20	16	10	82	61	76
6	Derby County	46	20	14	12	69	54	74
7	Middlesbrough	46	20	13	13	49	41	73
8	Bristol City	46	19	13	14	59	53	70
9	Nottingham Forest	46	17	15	14	61	54	66
10	Swansea City	46	18	11	17	65	62	65
11	Brentford	46	17	13	16	73	59	64
12	Sheffield Wednesday	46	16	16	14	60	62	64
13	Hull City	46	17	11	18	66	68	62
14	Preston North End	46	16	13	17	67	67	61
15	Blackburn Rovers	46	16	12	18	64	69	60
16	Stoke City	46	11	22	13	45	52	55
17	Birmingham City	46	14	19	13	64	58	52*
18	Wigan Athletic	46	13	13	20	51	64	52
19	Queens Park Rangers	46	14	9	23	53	71	51
20	Reading	46	10	17	19	49	66	47
21	Millwall	46	10	14	22	48	64	44
22	Rotherham United	46	8	16	22	52	83	40
23	Bolton Wanderers	46	8	8	30	29	78	32
24	Ipswich Town	46	5	16	25	36	77	31

* Birmingham City were deducted nine points for breaching EFL profit and sustainability regulations.

Part Two: 2019/20

THE SEQUEL NOBODY WANTED, NOR WILL EVER FORGET

LIVING BIELSABALL

Popey and Whelan team news in,
The clues to the question, 'Will Leeds win?'
Fish and chips come rain or shine,
Down Beeston Hill the view's devine.

The gathered flock on Bremner Square,
Burgers and cigarette smoke-filled air.
Battered old turnstiles ruled by machine,
Eleven old turds polished by an Argentine.

Staring at the South Stand through the winter sun,
Waiting for a goal but the cheering doesn't come.
Hopes are raised, hopes are dashed, chances come and go,
Eddie, Eddie, chant the Kop as panic starts to grow.

Under the lights as the clock ticks down, all eyes on the board,
At least five minutes added time, how have Leeds not scored?
Time-wasting antics, stonewall pens, the Football League's corrupt,
Then suddenly the net does bulge, Elland Road erupts.

Three more points and top ut' league, everyone's delighted,
Our heroes take their honour lap, Leeds are so united.
Racing back up Beeston Hill, how the lads had fought,
The final word as every week, 'Thanks for your incredible support.'

We Go Again

LIKE MY father before me, I was not born a dyed-in-the wool Leeds fan. My dad grew up in the 1950s and fell in love with Spurs, but one trip to Elland Road was all it took for him to catch the bug and his youth was spent following Leeds up and down the country. Despite my dad being a Leeds fan, and all my grandparents being born and bred Loiners, I was actually pushed into supporting Everton by my brother on the morning of the 1989 all-Merseyside FA Cup Final. We were playing football in the garden and Gianni declared he'd be Liverpool and I'd be Everton, in a kickabout that would shape our lives.

From that day I was head over heels for Everton. There is a video of me at six years old, slumped over the radio in floods of tears with Everton on their way to another Merseyside derby defeat (the curse of the radio is a lifelong affliction). My first love was Tony Cottee. I wanted to marry him (according to my mum, unchallenged), and my highlight as an Evertonian was the famous 4-4 draw with Liverpool in an FA Cup replay in 1991, when Cottee scored equalisers in normal and extra time.

My first encounter with Leeds United had come a few weeks earlier, Liverpool away on New Year's Day 1991, although at the time it was more like Leeds at home as my dad and I were sat with Gianni and the Liverpool fans in the Main Stand. Liverpool were reigning First Division champions and beat Wilko's Second Division champions 3-0, my only memory being John Lukic scoring a diving header into his own net. That's how I remembered it, anyway.

By the time of my first visit to Elland Road I knew all the Leeds players. I'd been enthralled watching their 4-1 and 6-1 wins at Villa Park and Hillsborough live on ITV as Leeds battled with their old foes from Manchester in the title race. It was February 1992, Luton Town at home, courtesy of my dad's best friend who had two spare tickets in the South Stand. It was an unmemorable match, but both goals happened in front of us and a Frenchman called Eric Cantona sealed the win with a tap-in on his home debut. I was absolutely hooked. To steal some of that Frenchman's words, I don't know why, but I loved them.

I managed to get to two more games that season, a 5-1 thrashing of Wimbledon, and a 3-0 thrashing of Chelsea that kept Leeds's faint title hopes alive. However, the championship race swung dramatically over Easter, with the red devils crumbling under the weight of expectation from their starved, manic, and desperate fanbase. Howard Wilkinson's heroes held their nerve and were crowned champions of England, and supporting Leeds was all downhill from there.

Despite losing the title, Alex Ferguson still believed his team was the best in the country, and the following season they atoned for their Easter collapse by winning the league by ten points. Fast forward 27 years and Leeds had their own Easter collapse to atone for, although now there was even more than the weight of history to contend with. Andrea Radrizzani was spending £1.5m per month to cover the club's losses and it was widely accepted that without promotion he would have to cut his cloth accordingly; players would be sold, Marcelo Bielsa would leave. In 2018/19, El Loco's failure to overcome the tag of 'The Damned United' was an honourable defeat, but in the last-chance saloon of 2019/20, failure was unthinkable. As was the final hurdle that the Football Gods had been keeping up their sleeves since the club was formed 100 years ago.

Pre-season 2019/20

It was a funny old pre-season. El Loco was here, so priority number one had already been achieved. So too was the linchpin of the team, Kalvin Phillips, who let his heart rule his head and rejected lucrative offers from the Premier League for one last chance to get there with his boyhood club.

Bielsa named four transfer targets, three of whom were promptly delivered; Jack Harrison was re-loaned from Manchester City, a young centre-back called Ben White was loaned from Brighton, and Hélder Costa arrived from Wolves in a deal that would cost Leeds £16m, a true marquee signing. The fourth target was Liverpool's young winger Ryan Kent, but Kemar Roofe's sudden exit to Anderlecht changed the club's priorities and director of football Victor Orta instead put all his efforts into signing Arsenal's prodigious striker, Eddie Nketiah. Having been cruelly denied major signings in both of last season's transfer windows (Harvey Barnes in the summer, Dan James in the winter), Orta was ecstatic to get Nketiah to U-turn on his move to Bristol City and join Leeds instead (on loan, of course).

It all sounds very rosy, but there had been casualties. Last season's top scorer, Roofe, left for the Belgian league, while young starlet Jack Clarke signed for Tottenham, and Bailey Peacock-Farrell left 'for first-team football', joining Premier League Burnley as back-up to their reserve goalkeeper. But the biggest story of the summer was the shock departure of Pontus Jansson, not for tens of millions to the Premier League, but for a measly £5m to measly Brentford. Pontus was a cult hero at Elland Road and arrived when the club was still in disarray, but just a few minutes into his debut he celebrated a meaty tackle in front of the Kop as if he'd scored a goal, and everything seemed to change. The big Swede was pivotal in reconnecting the fans with their team, and his 'Magic Hat' song will go down in folklore, especially in my family as my dad went viral when adding verses and posting his version of the song online. Although there was plenty of mutual respect, Jansson and Bielsa were clearly not a match made in heaven and both parties were happy to split at the first opportunity. Some fans were angry at the summer business, criticising a net gain of £20m, but Bielsa had exactly the squad he wanted, and his word is gospel.

There are many signs of the progress the club has made under Andrea Radrizzani's ownership; a world-class manager, multimillion-pound signings, being favourites for promotion to the Premier League, and now you could add the pre-season schedule to the list as Leeds headed to Australia to play Manchester United in the grand opening of Perth's Optus Stadium, in front of 55,000 spectators. Only five years earlier Leeds's Romanian pre-season opponents hadn't bothered turning up for a match in Italy, leaving the team to play themselves. In the other game of that tour Leeds beat a pub team 16-0, with their goalkeeper swapping sides towards the end to get some practice.

Over 5,000 Leeds fans made the trip to Australia – a mind-blowing number – joining thousands more who resided on the other side of the world to significantly outnumber the plastic Manchester United fans. Marcelo Bielsa initially remained in Yorkshire, helping his new players get accustomed to Bielsaball, and helping the internationals, who were given extended breaks, get up to fitness. It wasn't until the eve of the match that The Great Man headed down under, and he spent the whole flight watching footage of the Australian training sessions he'd missed – classic El Loco. The next day, Leeds were hammered 4-0. Talk about a long journey home.

During the last week of pre-season I finally brought myself to rewatch the heartbreaking play-off second-leg defeat, and was taken aback by how well Leeds had played. They were terrific! Apart from the four hideous goals conceded (minor detail), it was one of their best performances of the season and reinforced my belief that Leeds were getting better and better under Bielsa. Also, what a match! It had to be the most thrilling and dramatic 90 minutes I have ever witnessed, and despite being on the losing side you have to be thankful when your team can produce such scintillating football, and memories that will last a lifetime.

I was now convinced that this season would produce only glorious memories, of Leeds United's return to the Premier League, Marcelo Bielsa's victory over the Football Gods, and maybe even the exorcism, once and for all, of the gypsy curse Don Revie claimed had been placed upon The Damned United.

August 2019

Bristol City 1-3 Leeds United

Just like last year, I double-booked myself for the opening weekend of the season, though this time it was due to an act of lameness. I had been waiting for the fixtures to be released before booking a trip away for Frankie's birthday, but one morning, only days before they came out, the situation slipped my mind and I booked a weekend in the Lake District, Friday to Sunday. I realised my mistake almost immediately, and spent the next few days hoping and praying that Sky moved Leeds's opening game to Sunday, or at least that they got an away game. Both my prayers were answered, so I was able to get to the pub in good time ahead of a 4.30pm Sunday kick-off without impacting Frankie's weekend. I was brimming with confidence and boldly predicted a 5-0 win for Leeds.

It would take Hélder Costa a few weeks to be 'Bielsa-ready', so apart from Ben White replacing Pontus Jansson, it was as you were from last season. Kiko Casilla took that sentiment a little too far and, just six seconds into the new season, was dribbling around the Bristol City striker in his own six-yard box. In the context of how last season finished I should have been fuming, yet once my jaw was off the floor I couldn't help but raise a smile at a quite astonishing exhibition of his cojones.

Kiko would have quite the afternoon, crazily rushing out of goal on more than one occasion, punching his captain square in the face, and making some good saves too. He also conceded what looked a pretty soft goal at his near post, but by that point Leeds were 3-0 up and cruising. Pablo opened the scoring, bending the ball beautifully into the top corner with his weaker left foot, then after half-time he conjured up the second goal, jinking past O'Dowda and planting the ball into the net off Patrick Bamford's forehead. Leeds were rampant, and when a counterattack ended with a tap-in for the resurgent Jack Harrison, my 5-0 prediction looked on. The goal conceded took some wind out of Leeds's sails, but while the last 15 minutes were nervy for all fans, for the neutrals the game was long dead.

Leeds had given an emphatic answer to anyone wondering whether they had the physical and mental strength to go again after the physical and mental pain of last season. They looked refreshed and focused, delivering a near-perfect opening-day performance that fired them to the top of the league. Catch us if you can!

Leeds United 1-1 Nottingham Forest

Leeds vs Forest is a big fixture no matter what division it's played in, mainly due to one man, whose 44 days in charge at Elland Road inspired a best-selling book, a blockbuster film, and Leeds's 'Damned United' moniker. In the 1970s Brian Clough made no secret of his disdain for Don Revie's Leeds team, but when Don left, Clough followed the age-old advice; if you can't beat 'em, join 'em. He said he wanted a crack at the European Cup, but Clough's actions suggested sabotage. Perhaps he took the age-old advice to sadistic levels; if you can't beat 'em, join 'em, ruin 'em, and then beat 'em. Following his sacking, The Damned United entered a long period in the wilderness, while Clough went to Nottingham Forest and won the European Cup, twice.

Justin accompanied me and my dad on the car journey and all three of us were confident that Leeds would walk the league this season. There was no blazing sunshine to welcome us back to Elland Road, but everything else was just as it should be at the start of a new campaign; beautiful fish and chips and a stadium full of hope and excitement. Leeds took total control of the game straight away, Harrison causing havoc down the left, Dallas causing havoc down the right, despite them being two of last season's weaker performers. Chance after chance went begging, but after an hour of probing the deadlock was finally broken when Klich's defence-splitting pass found Pablo Hernández, who took it on his chest and steered his finish calmly past the keeper.

Leeds continued their domination, but with 15 minutes to go Harrison was replaced by Alioski and suddenly all the impetus was lost, so much so that it came as no real surprise when Forest equalised. It was one of the scrappiest goals I've ever seen at Elland Road, a corner that bounced around the box like a hot potato before Lewis Grabban sliced wildly at the ball, making just enough contact to trickle it beyond the keeper, the despairing lunges of three Leeds defenders, and in off the post. On came Costa who brought a new threat, but the push for a winner boiled down to three penalty claims. The first would have been soft but the second was clear as day, and by the time Costa was shoved over in injury time the officials had dug their heels in so deep they'd have felt silly changing tack.

The final whistle blew as Costa set off on another dangerous run down the wing, bringing Elland Road together in a chorus of obscenities. As always, Bielsa would not be drawn into criticising the ref; instead he bemoaned the continuation of last season's efficiency problem, but there was no doubt it had taken a combination of the two to deny Leeds victory.

Wigan Athletic 0-2 Leeds United

I was in Texas with work when Kinky Dave offered up two spare tickets for the weekend trip to Wigan. Lewis was back from Canada, so this presented us with the chance to go to our first away game together in a decade, since the night Gareth Bale got no change out of Jason Crowe, and Luka Modrić spent 90 minutes in Michael Doyle's pocket. Lewis immediately approved the notion, so I snapped Kinky's hand off before addressing the elephant in the room; my heavily pregnant wife (pardon the unfortunate pun). Frankie had been home alone all week, and wasn't happy to hear I would only be home for two hours before shooting off again, but she gave her blessing, as I knew she would. She is a very understanding wife, and highly respectful of the 'Bielsa card' that I always play in these situations. When he is gone I may regret playing it so fervently.

Considering who Leeds were playing today, it was impossible not to think about that godforsaken Good Friday. 'I could talk a lot about our 2-1 defeat, but that is not why we are here,' said Bielsa. Marcelo was right. Today was not a revenge mission; winning couldn't even begin to fix those wounds, only promotion would. Nevertheless, the Football Gods were doing their best to remind us of that fateful day when, midway through the first half, Wigan were reduced to ten men. Leeds were getting back on the horse. The parallels continued as Patrick Bamford then opened the scoring. Surely this time they would see the job through.

In the second half the Leeds fans were cheering a certain penalty when a gentle cross was palmed behind by a Wigan defender. It was impossible not to give, the linesman was yards away and the referee was looking right at it, but only a corner was awarded. 'And now you're gonna beliiieeeve us … The Football League's corrupt!' The chant was still in full flow when incredulation turned to jubilation as Bamford bundled the resulting corner into the net. Who needs VAR when the Football Gods can hand out justice so swiftly? The rest of the game was a frustrating procession. Every five minutes Leeds were creating and missing glorious chances to add to the lead, but at the final whistle they had their three points and were back on top of the league.

El Loco wouldn't place any significance on the fact that Leeds were top, of course; it was just a pleasing start. I hoped the fans would take heed, having ludicrously turned a third of last season into a series of 'must-win' matches. This season, Leeds were just 43 cup finals from glory.

Leeds United 1-0 Brentford

Wigan followed by Brentford – even the fixture list was mocking us! It was a replica of the Easter weekend that cost Leeds promotion, but thanks to their superb start to the season nobody even seemed to notice. It's amazing what a few good results can do. The big story of this game was the return of Pontus Jansson, a player Bielsa declared the best in the squad, both before and after he threw him on the scrapheap. The photo of Pontus signing for Brentford was telling; he looked perplexed and heartbroken to be signing for the West London minnows. I still loved Jansson, and always will, as he's a great bloke, so passionate about football, a true fan at heart, and a great defender. I was expecting him to be on fire for his big return and, fuelled by pre-match pints in The Boathouse, my mates all agreed it would be a great idea to each stick £25 in a pot to win £5,000 if Pontus was to score the opening goal.

It turned out to be a low-key return for the big Swede and a few half-hearted boos greeted his first few touches, but he had a decent game and for 80 minutes that was good enough. However, as Brentford's ambition shrunk, Leeds started to turn the screw, and in the closing stages Bielsa did what he wasn't able to do for the majority of last season, introduce pace and quality from the bench. Hélder Costa and Eddie Nketiah each possess both. Chants of 'Eddie, Eddie, Eddie' were already ringing out when the Arsenal loanee was warming up, then the noise intensified when he came on, and just four minutes after that came the crescendo as Costa flew down the wing and laid the winning goal on a plate for Nketiah to tap into the net. In Eddie, a star was born, in Costa a star had been added, and the man who signed both players, Victor Orta, celebrated more emphatically than anybody inside Elland Road, smashing up his monitor in the directors' box in sheer passion. At the final whistle Jansson hugged all his old team-mates, then marched straight down the tunnel, head down, ignoring the playful goads of a jubilant South Stand, who were imploring him to do his traditional victory fist pump.

On Instagram the next day, Pontus posted a photo of himself leading Brentford out of the tunnel, wearing that same look of sad bemusement that he wore when he signed for them. I felt a similar sadness. For three years I'd dreamed of Pontus taking Leeds to promotion, parading the Championship trophy around Elland Road. I'd declared Jansson the saviour of Leeds United but, in the end, the biggest cheer he got on his return to Elland Road was when Nketiah won a corner off him.

Stoke City 0-3 Leeds United

Nathan Jones was appointed as Stoke manager in the week of Bielsa's legendary PowerPoint presentation, when The Great Man laid bare his obsessive pre-match preparations in the wake of the Spygate fiasco. Jones claimed to have outsmarted Bielsa by switching to a formation he had never used before, and with the help of the referee Stoke claimed a 'famous' 2-1 victory. A photo of the momentous occasion was instantly hung in the corridors of the stadium; Nathan Jones with arms outstretched, Marcelo Bielsa crouched in defeat alongside him. Stoke had only won two league games out of 22 since, and Jones was on the brink.

Leeds finally picked up their first injuries of the season in the lead-up to this top-against-bottom clash. With three of the back four missing, Leeds lined up with two wingers at full-back, a right-back at centre-back, and 21-year-old loanee Ben White. Normally this would be cause for panic, but Bielsaball doesn't rely on specialists or specifics and Leeds controlled the game throughout, taking a first-half lead thanks to some mesmeric one-touch football. The beauty was in the assist, the wizardly vision and world-class execution of Pablo Hernández's through ball, but almost as impressive was the fact it was right-back Stuart Dallas who had burst beyond the Stoke defence to finish the move.

In the second half Leeds upped their game and didn't have to wait long for the second goal. Long, patient build-up play sprang into life on the edge of the box, Bamford provided a lovely ball into the corridor of uncertainty, and this time it was left-back Gjanni Alioski who burst beyond the Stoke defence to apply the finishing touch. Leeds were at their imperious best, and the third goal again came courtesy of Hernández's genius. His 40-yard daisy-cutter opened Stoke up again and Bamford was on hand to seal the points. Nathan Jones is a devout Christian but he must have wondered why his God had forsaken him when he saw Hélder Costa and Eddie Nketiah stripped off and ready to enter the fray, and with the super-subs introduced Leeds tore through Stoke at will. However, some great saves, some wasted chances, and perhaps some divine intervention kept the final score at 3-0.

Regardless of all the fantastic attacking play, there was only one candidate for the man of the match award – Ben White. Having only previously appeared in the lower leagues, nobody expected White to be a competent replacement for Pontus Jansson – who had just appeared in a World Cup quarter-final against England – but he'd taken to the Championship like a duck to water, or more fitting, a swan. Today he was magnificent, showing a similar grace and composure that a young Rio Ferdinand brought to the Leeds defence 20 years earlier. For all Jansson's character, his passion to defend and physical prowess, he was limited on the ball, and with two centre-backs who could play football Leeds now had even greater control of matches. Bielsa warned that we would find out the true quality of White in his reactions to mistakes. That's if he ever made any.

Leeds United 0-1 Swansea City

The last week of August was an improbable carbon copy of last season. Both started with a 3-0 away win and ended with a first vs second clash at Elland Road, with an EFL Cup defeat to the Championship's bottom club sandwiched between. This season's cup defeat was at the hands of Stoke, inflicting instant revenge for Saturday's mauling and earning Nathan Jones a stay of execution. Yet the victorious Potters didn't even win as Leeds fought back from 2-0 down but couldn't force the winner and lost on penalties. There had been 30,002 in attendance, giving me and the McTague brothers the great satisfaction of pushing the attendance over the 30,000 mark for a meaningless game, but one that I'll never forget.

It was an entertaining match and an atmosphere that most clubs would be proud of on a Champions League night, but these were not the reasons this match will live long in the memory. I'd bought tickets right behind the home dugout, as near to Bielsa as I could calculate, and of course I was fixated on El Loco throughout. It was such a thrill to be so close to The Great Man, and fascinating to see his staff up close and personal, as they were almost as energetic and passionate as the players. The big surprise was how many arguments Bielsa engaged in with the fourth official (considering how respectful he is towards officials in his post-match pressers), although they always ended with an apologetic raised hand and a nod of acceptance. Bielsa was gutted after an epic penalty shoot-out, but I was happy enough to concentrate on the league, and happier still that extra time had been abolished in the EFL Cup, meaning the players were nice and fresh for their top-of-the-table clash.

The Championship's top two had almost identical records – Leeds ahead by one goal scored – but it wasn't yet known whether Swansea were actually good or just having a good start. Leeds raced out of the blocks, creating five chances in the first 15 minutes, but at half-time it remained 0-0, something we'd become accustomed to and therefore it was nothing to fear. However, as time ticked on in the second half the atmosphere became more and more agitated. Leeds's broken-down attacks frustrated the crowd, Swansea's antics frustrated the crowd, and the referee frustrated the crowd. Costa and Nketiah were introduced to push Leeds over the line, but Eddie missed the golden chance of the match, heading into the side netting of an open goal, albeit from a tight angle. Just when Leeds seemed destined to replicate last August's 0-0 draw with Middlesbrough, Swansea won a 90th-minute corner. It was only half cleared and the recycled ball found Wayne Routledge in the middle of the box, where his scruffy finish bobbled into the corner of the South Stand net. The definitive smash-and-grab.

Bielsa remained very calm in his post-match presser; he knew results would reflect the performances come what may, but for the mere mortals it was a gut-wrenching way to go into the international break. The consolation prize, similar to the Forest game, was knowing that Swansea were not the real deal. They may have achieved the perfect result, but on another day they'd have been blown away and had no complaints. This was another team that would surely pose no threat to Leeds's promotion bid.

September 2019

1	Swansea	16
2	Charlton	14
3	**Leeds**	**13**
4	West Brom	12
5	Bristol City	11
6	Fulham	10

Barnsley 0-2 Leeds United

International breaks are always long, especially the first one of the season, and particularly when you've just lost a top-of-the-table clash. So the first Yorkshire derby of the season being moved back to Sunday was the icing on an overbaked cake, and it was 15 September when the second month of the season finally commenced. Swansea had lost the day before, continuing the non-coincidental sequence of teams beating Bielsa and losing their next match, thus Leeds had the chance to go straight back to the top of the table with a win at Oakwell.

I was in Amsterdam for a trade show with work and spent the first half glued to my phone as my dad sent updates via text. It seemed to be an exciting, full-blooded derby, as every few minutes I would receive a message about another Leeds chance gone begging, and Barnsley were missing chances too. At half-time it was 0-0 and now I had a meeting that would last the whole second half. I managed to get through the meeting without checking my phone, all the while wondering what news would await me at the end. With Costa and Nketiah waiting in the wings I was confident Leeds would claim all three points, and as we walked out of the meeting room Chris broke the good news. '2-0 Leeds. Nketiah and Klich.' I was thrilled, but with my customers in tow I managed to limit my celebration to a semi-professional fist pump.

When the trade show finished for the day I headed straight into Amsterdam to meet up with Paul, who had popped over from The Hague. There was no limiting the celebrations now; Bielsa's boys were top of the league and all professionalism went out of the window. Rediscovering it for the final day of the show was no mean feat.

Leeds United 1-1 Derby County

Comments about the Wigan game notwithstanding, Derby's return to Elland Road couldn't possibly pass without half an eye on revenge. Leeds were robbed of a play-off final appearance on that fateful Wednesday night in May, and what else was robbed from us we will never know. Anything could have happened in the play-off final against Aston Villa, the two biggest clubs in the Championship at loggerheads, just weeks after that unforgettable dead rubber. Marcelo Bielsa had deserved to lead his team out at Wembley at the very least, but that was all in the past, just another chapter in our gloriously disappointing history.

It was no longer Frank Lampard's Derby County. Phillip Cocu was now in charge and not doing so well, as with one win all season the Rams were languishing in 19th place. I once again predicted a 5-0 win for Leeds, and they duly started like a house on fire. A supreme exhibition of high-intensity football resulted in a level of domination I'd never seen before. It's no exaggeration to report that Derby didn't get out of their own half until the 40th minute, and even that was brief. However, time and time again Leeds let their opponents off the hook through poor decisions, poor final balls, or poor finishing. They did manage to go in with a half-time lead, but only because Derby scored a calamitous own goal.

The onslaught continued in the second half and immediately Bamford hit the post with a five-yard sitter, then won a penalty after great work in the box. Mateusz Klich was handed the ball, fresh from converting from the spot at Barnsley. The Pole's super-cool penalty technique had never let him down before (not even in training, according to Kalvin Phillips), and Klich strolled confidently towards the ball. The keeper dived to the right, Klich rolled the ball to the left, but the net didn't bulge and his shot trickled a yard wide of the post. The crowd were stunned by the penalty miss and so were the players, whose intensity levels dropped and the tension rose as Derby worked their way back into the match. They brought on Chris Martin. 'He's bound to get a chance,' said my dad. 'And he'll tuck it away,' was my instinctively pessimistic response.

Derby had barely registered a shot all game, but as we entered injury time Leeds were panicking, and in the 92nd minute their first chance of the match fell to Martin, who tucked it away as expected. The sound of a late goal at Elland Road to steal points off Leeds is horrible, and the simultaneous banging of 8,000 Kop seats coupled with the ecstatic roar from the away end had now been heard in four of the last five home games. There was still time for a big penalty shout when Hélder Costa was cynically body-checked as he chased a one-two with fellow substitute Nketiah, but neither the ref nor linesman were interested in giving it, and it would probably have been missed anyway. From the sublime performance to the ridiculous finishing, these were two exasperatingly dropped points.

At his post-match press conference Bielsa wore a wry smile as he said, 'We don't need to have this press conference, we did it in the last match!' El Loco was a happy man. He said it was the best 60 minutes Leeds had played under him and couldn't understand how anyone could feel negatively. I did agree, but I was still gutted. On the way home we listened to Manchester City vs Watford on the radio, and inside 18 minutes City were 5-0 up on their way to an 8-0 victory. City may be on a different planet to Leeds, but it still twisted the knife. They were no more dominant than Leeds, they made no more chances than Leeds did, they just knew where the net was.

FIFA Fair Play Award 2019

Chris Martin's equaliser played heavily on my mind over the next few days, until a wonderful surprise greeted me when scrolling through Twitter on the Tuesday evening. Marcelo Bielsa and Leeds United had received the FIFA Fair Play Award for their sportsmanship in allowing Aston Villa to walk the ball into the net at the end of last season. FIFA explained that Leeds had surrendered automatic promotion by giving the goal away, which was only true mathematically; nevertheless, no person will ever deserve this award more than El Loco.

In the past year he had spent £3m on a new training complex for his first club, Newell's Old Boys, as a thank you for giving him the platform to launch his football career. He'd also insisted on paying the £200,000 fine for the Spygate fiasco out of his own pocket, and bought a car for the club to give away in the staff's Christmas raffle. These gestures (and many more) would remain widely unknown, the fact his teams rarely show dissent to referees or try to deceive them would remain largely unnoticed, but Marcelo Bielsa's legacy now carried a fitting tribute, nonetheless.

Making this award even sweeter was the implication that the wider world saw the hysteria over Spygate for the farce it was. It made a mockery of our country's response to the story. Some sections of our media still had a laugh at the 'irony' of Bielsa winning it, some claimed to be outraged, while the EFL Twitter account just ignored it altogether, offering no congratulations whatsoever to one of their members who had received this prestigious global recognition. Sky Sports News also chose to turn a blind eye, failing to mention it despite dedicating nine minutes of airtime to the other winners. What a bunch of ignoramuses.

In his acceptance speech, Bielsa thanked his family, friends, and Newell's Old Boys for teaching him the correct way to behave, then praised the Leeds players, staff, and fans for accepting his decision to give the goal: 'Often the challenge is not knowing what is right and wrong, but accepting the consequences of doing the right thing.'

Marcelo Bielsa, a beacon of hope in a sport riddled with cheating, hypocrisy and greed.

Charlton Athletic 1-0 Leeds United

Lee Bowyer had made a great start to his managerial career, taking the club that launched his playing career back into the Championship amid boardroom chaos. Now he faced the club where he blossomed into one of the best midfielders in the country. I loved Bowyer, who was the heartbeat of the Leeds team that took Europe by storm at the turn of the century, and his vital goals against AC Milan, Barcelona, and Anderlecht took Leeds to within 90 minutes of the holiest of grails – a European Cup Final rematch with Bayern Munich at the San Siro. But on the eve of the semi-final second leg against

Valencia, UEFA inexplicably banned Bowyer for an alleged stamp in the goalless first leg at Elland Road. The incident was only allowed to be reviewed because legendary referee Pierluigi Collina didn't book Bowyer. He made the players shake hands instead. With the heart of the team ripped out Valencia triumphed 3-0 (only after the first goal was punched into the net. Damned or what?).

Harrogate was hosting the World Road Cycling Championships and I'd promised to take Frankie despite it clashing with the Charlton game, with Frankie promising we'd be back for the second half. I'd hoped to follow the first half via my dad's WhatsApp updates, but due to the massive crowds I couldn't get a signal, so it was an agonising wait to find out the half-time score. I finally received the bad news when I got home to my trusty(ish) wi-fi; Leeds were totally dominant, but losing. Midway through the half Kiko flapped at a ball that was floating into his chest, pushing it against the Charlton player's arse and back into the net, a real howler. In the second half Charlton employed all the usual spoiling tactics, while Leeds, without the injured Hernández, looked toothless and eventually clueless. A heroic goal-line block denied Forshaw a last-gasp equaliser, thus Leeds were condemned to their second defeat of the season, and dropped down to fourth place.

Out came the doom-mongers, emerging from their misery pits to spread online panic, and while I wasn't panicking myself, I was no longer of the mindset that Leeds would walk the league with 100 points. In order to do that they needed to eradicate the sloppiness in each box that plagued last season, but if anything the sloppiness was getting worse.

October 2019

1	West Brom	19
2	Swansea City	18
3	Nottingham Forest	18
4	**Leeds**	**17**
5	Preston	17
6	Charlton	17

Leeds United 1-0 West Bromwich Albion

Tonight was a first for Marcelo Bielsa. In his 62 games as Leeds manager, he had never faced a team currently ranked above him in the league. West Brom came to Elland Road as unbeaten league leaders so I was leaving nothing to chance, or looking at it another way, totally relying on chance. I don't believe in superstitions, but I have them just in case, so not only did I don my lucky Israel socks, I also resurrected my lucky green Bielsa top from last season, and my lucky grey jumper from Garry Monk's 2016/17 season. What could possibly go wrong?

Firstly, the traffic. Harrogate was still suffering the reverberations of the World Cycling Championships and it took forever just to get on to the A61. As we raced against time to make it to Park Fisheries before closing (making kick-off was a secondary concern), Radio Leeds broke the news that the FA were investigating an allegation that Kiko Casilla used racist language during the Charlton match. Kiko would remain available for selection until the case was heard, but nevertheless this was a potentially toxic distraction.

Rising to the challenge of playing the league leaders, Leeds were at their vibrant best in the first half and took a deserved lead when Alioski drove Harrison's perfectly weighted lay-off into the bottom corner. There was a golden opportunity to double the lead in first-half stoppage time, but Bamford poked straight at the keeper from five yards, thus regret lingered throughout the break. Nevertheless, it had been a very good half against the most adventurous and dangerous team Leeds had faced this season.

Tyler Roberts was introduced at half-time, in place of the impressive but injured Jamie Shackleton. With the game developing into a manic, end-to-end affair, Roberts suffered the indignity of being substituted himself just 20 minutes later in a ruthless decision by Bielsa, one that he apologised profusely for after the match (well, he apologised for bringing him on, not taking him off!). On came Ayling, returning from injury to shore up the defence, and the ever-improving, ever-versatile, ever-willing, and ever-present Stuart Dallas moved from full-back to shore up the midfield. The change worked and Leeds regained control, aided by a colossal display by Patrick Bamford, who dominated two strong centre-backs all night. A late West Brom bombardment was successfully repelled, and when the final whistle blew players from both teams collapsed to the floor, joy and despair united by exhaustion. It had been a great advert for the Championship, a division that Marcelo's boys were top of once again.

Having taken his share of the blame when similar tactical reinforcements backfired against Forest and Derby, I was delighted that El Loco's changes had paid off tonight. With 20 points from the first ten games Leeds were a point better off than last season, but all was not quite rosy again, not with the dreaded trip to Millwall next on the fixture list.

Millwall 2-1 Leeds United

Like many others I'm sure, each week I spend hours trying to work out what will happen in the upcoming match, and there was a lot of information to process in trying to second-guess whether Leeds would falter at The Den yet again. They had lost on nine of their last 11 trips to South Bermondsey and their recent record throughout London was even worse, with just one win in 16. Surely Leeds were due a win? But then Millwall hadn't won in eight games leading in to this match, and we know how much Leeds love breaking those runs for opponents. Then just two days before the game came the surprising news that long-term manager (four and a half years is genuinely a long-term spell nowadays) Neil Harris had stepped down. Would this galvanise Millwall further, or leave them totally hapless? Deep down, we all knew the answer.

I arrived home from visiting my in-laws ten minutes after kick-off. I put the kettle on and tuned in to *Soccer Saturday*, whose live updates banner instantly delivered terrible news: 'Red Card, Gaetano Berardi (Leeds)'. Worse still, Millwall also had a penalty, finished off as well as you will ever see, a thunderbolt right into the top corner. My despair turned to anger when seeing a replay of the incident. It's one thing to be fooled into a bad decision, and this was a clear dive by the Millwall attacker, but with Phillips stood in front of him ready to block any shot, giving a red card was beyond outrageous. Leeds responded well, and should have had a penalty of their own, but on the stroke of half-time Millwall made it 2-0, and in my defeatist head that was game over. Thankfully, Bielsa's team are not so easily defeated, and just 15 seconds in to the second half they pulled a goal back. Suddenly there was hope.

The ten men dominated the rest of the game, but despite an impressive 70 per cent possession they never really looked like equalising, so yet again Leeds headed in to an international break stewing over a defeat.

Leeds were now fifth in the table, the lowest position of Bielsa's reign, and after the match El Loco came as close to criticising the ref as he ever had: 'There were three important situations; the penalty, the red card, and the next situation when Harrison went down in the box. But I prefer to analyse the game and not the referee.'

The referee had more or less decided the game at the first sniff of an opportunity, but amid Leeds fan's claims of conspiracy, the reality of the situation was aptly summed up by Lewis in our post-match debrief, 'It's fair game to hate Leeds, always has been.' Berardi's red card was later rescinded, Leeds's first successful appeal in 12 years. There was no punishment for the Millwall diver, nor the referee.

Leeds United 1-0 Birmingham City

On Thursday, 17 October Leeds United celebrated its 100th birthday. It was a lovely day to be a Leeds fan, with uplifting eulogies by ex-players and supporters popping up on Twitter throughout, but the highlight had to be the sight of Marcelo Bielsa at the black-tie dinner in his Leeds tracksuit. Some people suggested he doesn't own any other clothes except his training gear, but I suspect he just didn't have time to get changed. He will have been busy turning the remaining stones to help his team cap off the celebrations with three important points.

Unlike my considerate unborn son, we arrived early, and it was a carnival atmosphere both outside and inside the ground. Legends lined the pitch in the lead-up to kick-off, then we were 'treated' to Premier League-style razzmatazz, with fireworks and a mural welcoming the current players from the tunnel. Hopefully this wasn't an indication of what awaits in the Promised Land; once every 100 years is enough for me. Elland Road was electric and the players, in Don Revie's classic kit and El Loco's classic 3-3-1-3 formation, responded with a wonderful first-half performance, but they couldn't force the opening goal.

As he was fresh from a hat-trick for England's under-21s, calls for Eddie Nketiah to replace Bamford in the team were getting louder, but when Eddie took over from Bamford for the second half it coincided with Leeds losing their grip on the match. Birmingham were on top and growing in confidence when The Great Man replaced Klich with Roberts in an attempt to reassert authority, and five minutes later Leeds took the lead. The goal was scored by The Yorkshire Pirlo, on a rare foray into the box due to his more advanced role in today's tweaked formation. When the ball hit the net the roar was glorious, and so too was Phillips's beaming smile as he jumped for joy before being mobbed by the players and substitutes. The last 20 minutes were spent anxiously clinging on to the narrow lead, but with Ayling and Berardi on top form either side of the unflappable Ben White, Leeds held firm to the final whistle. Blue and yellow glitter rained on to the pitch as the players celebrated, and Leeds were back in the top two.

There was nobody more fitting to claim the winning goal in the centenary match, not least because Phillips had been ill during the week and sacrificed his attendance at the black-tie dinner to ensure he was fit for the main event.

After the game, Bielsa was full of praise for Phillips in turning away the riches of the Premier League to stay with his beloved club, and for the divine intervention that rewarded him with a place in the history books forever: 'Sometimes God puts things in the right place.' Don't we just know it, Marcelo. He could have been speaking in the third person.

Preston North End 1-1 Leeds United

As Leeds crossed the Pennines for a midweek clash at Deepdale, a story broke from the Rugby World Cup in Japan. In the lead-up to the semi-final against New Zealand, England manager Eddie Jones told the press that a 'spy' had been caught filming their training session from a nearby building. Jones made light of it, saying he couldn't care less, that with all the analysis and data that is available nowadays there was no advantage to be gained, just as Bielsa had claimed during his famous PowerPoint presentation back in January. To the disbelief of absolutely nobody, there was no moral outrage, no investigation, and no six-figure fine for New Zealand. The story went no further.

No amount of spying can help you put the ball in the net, and this was another frustrating night for Leeds. They dominated throughout and created numerous chances, but the problem was that they mostly fell to the star striker. Outside the box Bamford was a major part of Leeds's superb play, but when it came to scoring goals he was really struggling. Five chances of varying difficulty came and went without drawing a save from the keeper, and even when opportunities fell to other players Leeds still couldn't score. Then in the closing stages they were hit by a sucker-punch, conceding on the counterattack having thrown one too many players forward.

Staring down the barrel of a third straight away defeat, Bielsa immediately swapped Bamford for Nketiah, and after ten minutes of huff and puff Leeds grabbed a late equaliser. Nketiah was the saviour, leaping like a salmon and looping a magnificent header over the keeper and beyond three Preston defenders on the goal line. A great goal, and a great relief.

The equaliser triggered a frenetic final five minutes and Leeds bombarded Preston, but either side could have won it at the death. In the last minute a Preston free kick was headed inches wide, then in the last seconds Roberts was sent tumbling in the box but the ref said no penalty. I really couldn't be bothered with any more injustice so I was pleased when replays showed that the defender did get the ball, although I still felt a little aggrieved as it was a very scruffy lunge. You've seen them given, but not for Leeds.

Despite dropping more points I wasn't going to lose any sleep. I couldn't ignore the fact that Leeds looked a much stronger team than last season. They were dominating every opponent and playing brilliant football, but if you can't score goals I suppose you can't be a brilliant side. After the match I watched highlights of the midweek action throughout the leagues. It was goal after goal after goal. Cross, header, goal. Curler from outside the box, goal. One-on-one with the keeper, goal. How were these other teams doing it? Even the worst teams in League Two were scoring goals, so why couldn't Leeds? The main culprit for the lack of goals had received unwavering support from the terraces all season, but tonight it felt like the camel's back had been broken, if not by the chances Bamford had missed, then by the metaphorical straw of Eddie's wonderful header.

Sheffield Wednesday 0-0 Leeds United

For the second time in a week I sacrificed the chance of a rare away ticket due to the imminent arrival of my unborn son, but at least today's game was fully televised as opposed to the midweek Red Button coverage. Replays and Don Goodman, who could want for more? The pre-match talk was dominated by the Bamford vs Nketiah debate, but unsurprisingly Bielsa stuck by Bamford, so Eddie would once again have to impact the game from the bench.

Top spot was up for grabs for the winners of this Saturday lunchtime Yorkshire derby, but at a sodden Hillsborough there was a dampened atmosphere, and even the Leeds fans sounded subdued. On the pitch it was a tight game but a decent and competitive battle. In the first half Kiko pulled off a wonderful top-corner save to deny Fletcher, while at the other end Westwood pulled off a wonderful bottom-corner save to deny Bamford. The luckless striker did everything right and his header looked in all the way, so much so that even Frankie (making a rare and brief appearance in the lounge) let out a 'GET IN!', but somehow it didn't.

Bielsa replaced Bamford with Nketiah for the second half, but this coincided with Leeds losing control of the match, as it had against Birmingham. Nketiah still looked a threat, and his electric burst of pace created a chance for Harrison that was blocked on the line, then moments later Alioski crashed a header against the inside of the post. Wednesday hit the woodwork themselves and forced Kiko into another terrific top-corner save, so in the end nobody could have any qualms about the result. A decent point rounded off a decent week for Leeds, even though they remained outside the automatic promotion places. It was debatable who had the better of the match everyone wanted to talk about, but the result was the same; Bamford 0-0 Nketiah.

Leeds were a third of the way through the campaign and the results were almost identical to last season; four wins and a draw, followed by three wins in the next nine (both inconsistent runs coinciding with a Pablo Hernández injury). From this point in 2018/19 Leeds went on to win eight of the next ten games, a feat that looked a big ask for the current side, unless some divine intervention could change their luck in front of goal.

November 2019

1	West Brom	27
2	Preston	25
3	**Leeds**	**25**
4	Swansea City	25
5	Sheffield Wednesday	24
6	Bristol City	24

Leeds United 2-0 Queens Park Rangers

Alessandro Marcelo Dean arrived five hours and 40 minutes into his due date on Monday, 28 October. I had wondered whether labour would be more excruciating than watching Leeds, and as it happened it wasn't. After a shaky opening, Frankie settled nicely and completely controlled proceedings; the harder she pushed the more inevitable the result became, and the game was over long before any panic could set in. Compared to watching Leeds, who had scored two goals from their previous 107 shots in open play, it was a walk in the park. His arrival on the Monday gave me the maximum chance of making the QPR game. In fact, I didn't even consider my attendance in doubt, but that turned out to be very naive. When Saturday came, I had no choice but to sacrifice the match.

In his pre-match presser, Bielsa announced that Eddie Nketiah would make his first start of the season, citing an ankle injury to Patrick Bamford as the reason for the change. However, Nketiah picked up an injury in Friday's training session (rumoured to be a twisted testicle) so Bamford ended up playing after all, for the full 90 minutes. El Loco also threw in a tactical curveball, with expected left-back Stuart Dallas instead deployed as a man-marker on QPR danger man Eberechi Eze. According to my dad's live updates, nobody played left-back, though Bielsa would later explain (without a hint of humour) that Jack Harrison had played left-back, midfield, and left wing.

From all reports the City loanee did all three jobs superbly, and he extended his run of assists to five goals in a row by setting up the opener for Tyler Roberts, another player with everything in his locker except the stats to match his undoubted ability. It was a lovely finish, a controlled, first-time side-footer from the edge of the box, showing the rest of the squad how to do it, and reminding himself too; it was his first goal in 13 months. Harrison's run of assists ended in the second half, despite his best efforts. Starting in the left-back position, he ventured through midfield, found himself in the left-forward position, and tried to lay a chance on a plate for Klich. The pass was blocked, but the ball fell back into the assist machine's path, where his only option was to finish – and he did so with aplomb. Thus the Leeds fans were treated to a nerveless last ten minutes, and a victory that seemed as comfortable as delivering a baby.

It had been a momentous first Saturday for Alessandro, not that he'd remember it himself, of course. A World Cup Final defeat in the morning (albeit in rugby), a Leeds win and a Manchester United defeat in the afternoon (always a special double, if not so uncommon nowadays), and at the end of the day Marcelo's men sat proudly on top of the league again. Sweet dreams, son, it's not always like this.

Leeds United 2-1 Blackburn Rovers

Without the injury merry-go-round of last season, the 2pm team news had become a mundane event, even with El Loco no longer revealing his line-up in the pre-match presser. He ended the ritual in style earlier in the season, with possibly my favourite display of his dry humour to date. 'I cannot name the team before the game, as a supporter said I was giving away a lot to the opposition. But between you and me, it's the same team.' It was the same team again today, and with Nketiah injured for the next few weeks there was a weight off the shoulders of Patrick Bamford, despite heading into his 11th game since last finding the net.

Like every first half at Elland Road this season, the away team barely got out of their own half. However, today Leeds were sloppy in midfield and struggled to create any chances in a difficult first half-hour. But football is a funny old game and, despite the worst home performance of the season, Leeds raced into a two-goal lead. The first came from the penalty spot after Luke Ayling tumbled in the box and Patrick Bamford grabbed the ball, determined to break his duck. I wondered whether the stadium would laugh or cry if he missed, but thankfully we will never know as the keeper dived the wrong way and the ball hit the net. Elland Road let out a sigh of relief and Bamford let out a roar of delight, before being mobbed by his appreciative team-mates, who I'm sure were as thrilled as Pat himself.

Minutes later, with the weight of the world off his shoulders, Bamford provided a truly world-class assist, controlling a long Phillips ball over his shoulder with Bergkamp-like deftness, then laying into the path of Jack Harrison, who placed a careful finish in off the post with his weaker right foot. Ironically, if it had fallen on his left foot he probably would have blazed it into the South Stand. A comfortable victory seemed on the cards, until Blackburn scored a soft goal from a corner just before half-time.

Like every second half at Elland Road this season, it was a nervy affair. However, Leeds remained on the front foot, trying to put the game to bed. Since breaking into the starting 11 at Charlton, marquee signing Hélder Costa had struggled to impact games the way he had from the bench, but today he enjoyed his best game in a white shirt, his magical wing play proving a constant threat. Nevertheless, Leeds couldn't find another goal, and nor could Blackburn, who could barely muster an attack, with the threat of danger man Bradley Dack totally repressed by a masterly performance from Kalvin Phillips.

For the first time in seven attempts, Marcelo Bielsa's Leeds team headed into an international break with that winning feeling. 'When you win, more than being happy, you are calm. It is good in football to have a period of calm,' he said. The Great Man has a great knack of pointing out previously subconscious truths and Leeds could not be happy, still sitting in third place, but on the back of a victory there is never need for panic or inquisition.

Luton Town 1-2 Leeds United

No need for inquisition, but during an international break what else is there to do? Debate surrounded 'Expected Goals' (or xG), which calculates the quality of goalscoring opportunities to provide data on who 'deserved' to win a match. The xG league table had Leeds a whopping 18 points clear of actual league leaders West Brom, but did this prove they would eventually rise to the top, or highlight the reason they would fail to achieve promotion again? One thing was clear; no matter how much they dominated a match, Leeds were capable of losing to anyone, even the league's minnows, Luton Town.

Pablo Hernández signed a new contract during the international break and Bielsa celebrated by recalling his fit-again talisman to the team. Two more years of Pablo would take him beyond his 37th birthday, the same age that his predecessor, Gordon Strachan, called time on his illustrious Leeds career. Although Pablo never looks particularly happy, in defeat you could always see how desperate the little Spaniard was to get his hands on the Football League trophy the little Scot lifted in 1992.

Surprisingly it was Hélder Costa who made way for Hernández. Bielsa acknowledged that his performances were improving, but an eight-game run in the team had yielded no goals and no assists, so it was back to impact-sub duty for the £16m man.

Frankie escaped to the supermarket (apparently the equivalent of a holiday in the Maldives nowadays), leaving me and Alessandro to watch the game in peace. In the driving rain Leeds controlled the first half, Bamford diverted the best chance against the angle of post and bar, and Luton's keeper made great saves to deny Phillips, Harrison, and Roberts. At half-time I couldn't help thinking, 'Here we go again.'

Early in the second half Izzy Brown failed to con the referee on the edge of the Leeds box and Ben White carried the ball out of defence. White was still going 50 yards later, before releasing a beautiful defence-splitting pass with the outside of his boot, which Bamford drilled low into the net. Against such opposition the floodgates should have opened, but less than five minutes later it was 1-1 when Izzy Brown's peach of a cross was dispatched at the back post, with Luton's first shot on target. Then Luton scored again, only to be denied by a very late, and very incorrect, linesman's flag.

Leeds set about capitalising on their fortunate escape and the last half-hour was wave after wave of relentless attacks.

As the clock ticked down I remained surprisingly calm, able to take pleasure and confidence from the football Leeds were playing, and then in the 90th minute my calmness was broken as Klich's low cross was bundled past the keeper and into the corner of the net. Bamford tried to claim the goal, but the Dubious Goals Committee (they are a dubious lot) robbed him of it in the coming days.

There was a hearts-in-mouths ending as Luton missed a free header from eight yards out, but that was the last action and Leeds claimed a gritty victory that took them back into the automatic promotion spots.

I was bouncing off the walls after this win – 'The type of win that gets you out of this league,' according to legendary journalist Phil Hay. Bielsa would not be drawn into such headline statements, but his post-match comments were eerily topical: 'If you want to win, you have to fight. Deserving to win is not enough.' It was as if The Great Man had been reading all the mundane international-break chitter-chatter, and knowing him, he probably had.

Reading 0-1 Leeds United

Mark Bowen was looking for his fourth straight home win as Reading manager since making the rare move downstairs from the directors' box, while Leeds were looking for their fourth straight win since Alessandro was born. The New Manager Bounce vs The New Baby Bounce, and under the lights at the Madejski Stadium something had to give.

After a great opening ten minutes I WhatsApped my mates to praise the intensity of the team, but the 'commentator's curse' reared its ugly head as suddenly the intensity dropped and a scrappy half ensued. I was grateful in the end for half-time bagels, and in the second half Leeds regrouped and steadily improved, but so too did Reading. This was a much stronger side than the one Leeds had strolled past at the back end of last season.

I was preparing to settle for the draw that would keep the unbeaten run going when, in the 87th minute, Reading were awarded a free kick on the edge of the Leeds box. Kiko parried the well-struck shot away towards the corner flag, the follow-up cross was blocked by Dallas, and the loose ball fell to Jack Harrison. Where 99 per cent of footballers would have hoofed it down the line, Harrison played a clever reverse pass back into the path of Dallas, and the newly dubbed 'Cookstown Cafu' drilled a majestic first-time ball out to the right wing, where Alioski picked it up and fed Hélder Costa on the overlap. Meanwhile, Harrison was bombing up the left wing. He covered almost the full length of the pitch in 13.6 seconds, arriving in the six-yard box right on cue to head home a glorious winning goal from Costa's cross. With Alessandro asleep in my arms I found an inner strength which I can only compare to a mother giving birth, containing my elation to stillness and silence. Unfortunately (or fortunately), Costa's cross had taken a slight deflection, so this couldn't be considered for goal of the season, but it was a top-class counterattack, a goal worthy of winning any game.

Successive late away wins in a matter of days added to the belief that this really would be Leeds's year. The same had been said after successive late wins last Christmas, but this season felt different. There was no uncharted territory being trodden, no boundaries being pushed, just the best team in the Championship winning matches.

Leeds United 4-0 Middlesbrough

Having been reunited with Lee Bowyer in September, Leeds completed the double as Jonathan Woodgate brought his struggling and injury-ravaged Middlesbrough team to Elland

Road. Woodgate was an exceptionally talented defender, for me the greatest product from our famous Thorpe Arch academy (especially if you expel a certain Australian from the reckoning, which I have), and he was central to the rise and fall of 'O'Leary's Babies' at the turn of the century.

'Living the dream' all started when David O'Leary threw an 18-year-old Woodgate into the Leeds team, the first of an influx of youth players that transformed George Graham's well-oiled machine into a free-flowing bundle of joy. Then came the trial that cast a shadow over the club and eventually derailed Leeds altogether; Woodgate and Bowyer were charged with grievous bodily harm after a student was viciously attacked on a night out in Leeds. Both players were eventually cleared of GBH, but while Bowyer excelled on the pitch during the court proceedings, Woodgate became a shadow of himself and never fully recovered. By January 2003 the wheels had come off at Elland Road, O'Leary had been sacked, Leeds were sliding down the Premier League, and the most expensive signings had been sold. But for fans it was the sale of Woodgate to Newcastle that marked the end of the era; that was the moment we all knew 'the dream' was over.

Today was the day that Hélder Costa and Pablo Hernández finally started a game together, and what a start it was. Leeds were rampant. Bielsa's formation on paper had Ayling on the right of a three-man defence, but inside a minute 'Bill' was waltzing into the box and curling a left-footed shot inches wide. It set the tone, and four minutes later Bamford nodded home from close range to send the South Stand into raptures. My opinion on Bamford had transformed. The man I previously labelled 'languid' was now a machine; he had taken full advantage of Bielsa's training regime and was leading the line almost magnificently. If he could find his finishing touch consistently there would be no 'almost' about it.

Boro managed to weather the storm, but with the last attack of the half Bamford's hopeful cross was deflected into the path of Klich, whose weak shot was deflected into the net. I almost felt sorry for Woody as it was all going wrong for him at Elland Road, again.

A 2-0 lead is often described as a dangerous one, but in the second half Middlesbrough offered no resistance as Leeds romped to victory. The third arrived when Hélder Costa cut through two lame tackles and blasted past the keeper from 20 yards, and the goal glut continued when a short-corner routine left Klich with the space he needed on the edge of the box to curl an absolute peach into the top corner. We had a great view of it, and I'm sure I was the first in the ground to cheer. With Leeds having scored just one goal from almost 150 corners this season, after the game El Loco jokingly thanked Graham Smyth of the *Yorkshire Evening Post* for suggesting Leeds try more short corners. At least I think he was joking.

By the end I was a little disappointed that Leeds couldn't add more goals, but 4-0 was enough to send the required statement to their promotion rivals. The league was taking shape and Leeds and West Brom were sitting pretty, now five points clear of the chasing pack.

December 2019

1	West Brom	42
2	**Leeds**	**40**
3	Fulham	35
4	Nottingham Forest	33
5	Bristol City	32
6	Preston	31

Huddersfield Town 0-2 Leeds United

Leeds spent the week leading up to the West Yorkshire derby preparing centre-back Ben White to deputise for suspended midfielder Kalvin Phillips, but the contingency plan was thrown into chaos when White's defensive partner, Liam Cooper, was ruled out through injury on the morning of the game. Bielsa pressed on regardless, fielding his only available centre-back in midfield, with two wingers at full-back (Dallas and Alioski), and two full-backs at centre-back (Ayling and Berardi). Classic El Loco.

Leeds's problems paled into insignificance compared to their Yorkshire neighbours. On the back of a dismal relegation from the Premier League, Huddersfield had carried their poor form into this season and were only hovering above the relegation zone thanks to the points collected during a 'new manager bounce', having sacked their manager in mid-August (yes, August). Now they faced an injury crisis so severe that three teenagers had to be recalled from loans in non-league football in order to fill their bench. But this was their cup final, and throughout the first half the Terriers were full of beans, pressurising Leeds at every opportunity with an old-school 'up and at 'em' approach. Leeds gave as good as they got in the physical stakes but struggled to control the match in the absence of Phillips, so once again I was happy enough with the half-time bagels.

It was always going to be a big ask for Huddersfield to keep up their intensity for another 45 minutes, and just five minutes into the second half their spirit was broken when Alioski smashed home a volley from a half-cleared corner. Buoyed by the goal, Leeds found their mojo and started playing their lovely brand of controlled football. Huddersfield were chasing shadows, yet they came within inches of equalising when a point-blank header was blocked on the line by Casilla, and moments later Leeds launched another explosive counterattack. The ball was swept upfield with a poise and speed that simply does not belong in the Championship, culminating in a pinpoint Harrison cross for Pablo Hernández to nod in at the far post. Magnificent.

Bielsa's team was reaching new heights in all departments, the improvement typified by two players who had struggled last season. Jack Harrison had spent the summer in America, working on his game with specialist finishing coaches. The rewards were being reaped as he'd already matched his goals and assists output from last season. Stuart Dallas had refused to go on holiday at all, reporting for pre-season training straight after summer international duty in order to make sure he was Bielsa-ready from the get-go. Dallas was the only international to go on the Australia tour; now he was an automatic pick in the starting 11, be it at right-back, left-back, or in midfield.

Perhaps Kiko Casilla could also be put into that category as he could easily have jumped ship in the aftermath of his disastrous end to last season, but he was determined to stay at Leeds and finish the job he came to do. Kiko now had 11 clean sheets in 20 games this season, albeit thanks to Huddersfield missing three late sitters, kindly sparing a nervy finish.

Leeds United 2-0 Hull City

It was a wet and windy December evening, so, rather than walking, I gave myself a lift to the train station to meet Fan for our annual Christmas do. As I turned on the engine the car radio blared out, 'Don't you know pump it up, you've got to pump it up.' It was the first time I'd heard the pop song, but Leeds's adaptation, 'The whites are going up', had become a popular chant at Elland Road during the current winning sequence, so I took this as a good sign. It was a pitiful turnout for #LUCD2019, but neither attendee was bothered, especially with the Woollards due to meet us in Leeds to double the numbers. There was a nice festive atmosphere in The Boathouse as we drank pints and scoffed wonderful Christmas pizzas, though Big Steve Woollard missed the merriment due to traffic, only arriving in time to chauffeur us to the ground.

This was the third Yorkshire derby in a row (by historical borders anyway) and Leeds were looking to emulate last season's seven-game winning run. Hull were looking to emulate their shock victory at Elland Road, which ended that run, and started perfectly by winning the toss and making Leeds attack the Kop in the first half. Leeds struggled to create any clear chances despite total domination, so it was bagels again at half-time, washed down by rare half-time pints (Christmas do 'n that).

When Hélder Costa had a goal ruled out for offside, it was starting to feel like it wouldn't be Leeds's night, but after 74 minutes they finally broke the deadlock thanks to another own goal. Only Bamford had scored more goals for Leeds this season than the opposition. A few minutes later the victory was sealed with what could now be called a trademark counterattack. A free header from a corner (an unwanted trademark) brought a fantastic save from Casilla, then Bamford scrambled the loose ball away from the goal line, and 14 seconds later he arrived in the opposite box. The goal-cursed striker's cool side-footed finish only found the inside of the post, but Alioski smashed home the rebound from an acute angle. A delighted Elland Road hailed not the scorer, but the goalkeeper, with chants of 'KIKO, KIKO, KIKO!' From the start of the season the Leeds crowd had been eager to forgive Casilla for his sins that came at the cost of promotion, and Kiko himself was clearly keen to make amends. He had held his hands up in apology to the Kop before the first home game of the season, and tonight's gesture by the stand, effectively crediting him with the goal, felt like a closing of the loop. Half the players ran to Alioski and the other half ran to the Spanish keeper. It was a lovely sight.

West Brom had been going toe-to-toe with Leeds but finally flinched, drawing at Wigan to end their winning run at six and send Leeds back to the top of the league on goal difference. The chasing pack all failed to win and suddenly Leeds found themselves 11 points clear of the play-off places, the gap their performances deserved. Pundits across the land declared there was no stopping the current top two, but at Elland Road nobody was counting any chickens as Leeds had blown such gaps before. At the turn of the decade Leeds were top of League One, 20 points clear of Millwall with a game in hand, but by Easter they had dropped like a stone to fourth (before recovering to steal promotion by a point). In 2016/17 they missed out on a play-off place having been nine points clear of Fulham with eight games to go, and of course there was last season, when they were ten points clear of Sheffield United on Boxing Day but finished six points adrift of them. We knew all too well that things can change very quickly in the Championship.

Leeds United 3-3 Cardiff City

On a bitterly cold December afternoon I sacrificed my lucky Israel socks for the warmth of my kilt socks, retained from Nige's wedding in Edinburgh. Perhaps complacency was sneaking in, or perhaps subconsciously I sensed a bad result and didn't want to break the illusion of owning magical, match-winning socks. At Park Fisheries we were served the cursed double-fish, bringing doubt into my thoughts, but at least it wasn't raining. Then as we took our seats in the outdoor 'restaurant' the heavens opened. I began to regret having slightly warmer feet.

Had it occurred to me who would be in the opposition dugout I wouldn't have thought twice about donning my Israel socks. Neil Harris had recently taken over at Cardiff and always seemed to get the better of Leeds, as a player and a manager. It felt a lifetime ago, but it was less than two years since his Millwall team came to Elland Road and were two goals and a man up at half-time. An incredible fightback by Leeds was the highlight of the season, but the ten men couldn't hang on to their 3-2 lead as Millwall prevailed 4-3 with two late goals, the worst moment of a terrible season. Maybe it wasn't Harris that was the bogey, maybe it was just Millwall. Or maybe it was both.

Within two minutes of kick-off my sock selection was firmly at the back of my mind when another stunning counterattack was finished off by Hélder Costa, but Pablo Hernández received the plaudits, as his sumptuous 50-yard volleyed cross-field through ball was a thing of sheer beauty.

Inside ten minutes it was 2-0. Swarmed by white shirts, Cardiff lost possession in their own box and Bamford took Dallas's cross on his chest and fired a half-volley into the roof of the net almost in one smooth movement, a wonderful finish. Leeds were on fire, their football was sublime, and with their scoring boots on it felt world-class. Okay, it was only a Championship match, but Cardiff were a Premier League team just six months previously and they must have been as happy as Leeds with the 2-0 half-time scoreline, such was the home side's dominance. But nobody could have been as happy as Leeds with the half-time league table as they were a mind-boggling 14 points clear of third.

Early in the second half Bamford scored his fifth goal in seven games from the penalty spot. 'That's game over now,' declared Dave next to me. I didn't totally agree. I'm rarely calm at 3-0 as one goal could change the whole game, but I nodded in agreement, not wanting to dampen the joyfulness of the moment. Minutes later, Klich's delicate chip came within inches of making it 4-0 and the buoyant Kop mocked the Welsh visitors. Minutes after that the game turned.

Cardiff's lifeline came from an innocuous cross that drew Kiko needlessly to the edge of his box. He could only flap the ball into the path of Lee Tomlin, whose exquisite lob found the unguarded far corner of the net. With eight minutes remaining Cardiff scored again, a free header from a free kick, 3-2. Panic stations. Everyone in the ground expected the worst, and even when Cardiff were reduced to ten men for a wild lunge on Nketiah, that didn't calm any nerves, and Bielsa was feeling the heat too. He sent on young defender Pascal Struijk in place of Berardi for some extra height, but Struijk had only played two minutes of first-team football in his whole career, and sadly his inexperience showed. He was caught flat-footed as Tomlin continued his uncanny Zlatan Ibrahimović impersonation with an audacious backheeled through ball, which was scuffed passed Casilla and rolled into the net. Three shots on target, three goals, 3-3. Despite having expected the worst, Elland Road was stunned into silence.

Deep into injury time came a chance to prevail 4-3, as Harris had done in near identical circumstances for Millwall. It fell to Eddie Nketiah, but his downward header was parried by the keeper, the ball rebounded against Ben White, and trickled agonisingly wide before he could lunge to divert it home. The final whistle blew and the seat in front of me received the full wrath of my right boot, one kick for each of my emotions; anger, disappointment, disbelief.

A draw after a seven-game winning run is no disaster, but the manner of the result sent shivers down my spine. Leeds had imploded, just like in last season's play-offs. They had thrown away points from an unassailable position, just like in last season's run-in, their mental frailties laid bare for all to see. They still had a ten-point lead in the automatic promotion spots, but it was vital they responded quickly, to brush this result under the carpet and show the rest of the Championship that this was not the start of a 'typical Leeds' collapse.

Fulham 2-1 Leeds United

Leeds headed to the capital to face a Fulham side who were on the back of four straight defeats. Despite their form, the calls for manager Scott Parker's head and the 12-point gap to Leeds, Fulham were still considered the main danger to the promotion push; they had the most expensive squad in the division and the best striker, Aleksandar Mitrović. Keeping them at arm's length was imperative and a draw would do nicely today.

I had a Christmas engagement that clashed with the match, as my brother and his girlfriend had come all the way from

Japan to meet Alessandro, so *Soccer Saturday* stayed on mute and I cracked open the Prosecco. Before I'd poured out four glasses the inevitable flashed up: '1-0 Fulham, Mitrović (pen)'. When I saw the incident on Twitter I was once again seething, it was almost as soft as the Millwall debacle. Ben White's hand had brushed the striker's back as a high cross looped harmlessly over their heads, the Fulham man fell to his knees and the ref pointed to the spot before any players had even appealed. At least White didn't receive his marching orders.

In the second half we opened the mulled wine, and the accompanying mince pies tasted all the sweeter when Matt Murray reported a Leeds equaliser through Patrick Bamford, his tenth of the season, now a respectable total. Leeds pressed for the winner, but after sleeping through the whole match, Alessandro woke up to the first defeat of his life thanks to a thunderous Fulham goal 15 minutes from time. Leeds had chances to equalise, but a 95th-minute goal-line clearance by Mitrović sealed the home win. Fulham were up to third and the gap was down to nine.

I felt surprisingly calm about the defeat as we were now at the halfway point in the season and nine points was a fantastic lead. But the following day Sheffield Wednesday cut the gap to eight and suddenly I was panicking again. With tough trips to Birmingham and West Brom to come, Leeds had to get a win at Elland Road on Boxing Day, for my own sanity if nothing else.

Leeds United 1-1 Preston North End

In the pre-match press conference Bielsa revealed that Pablo Hernández would be out for a month, a hammer blow at a stage of the season when fixtures against their promotion rivals were coming thick and fast. Having missed all but 40 seconds of the defeat at Fulham (fourth in the table), Hernández would now be absent against Preston (fifth), West Brom (first), and Sheffield Wednesday (third) over the next two weeks. Last season Pablo was virtually an ever-present, minus a block of seven games during which Leeds only won twice, and only scored more than one goal once. This season he had already missed a block of six games, during which Leeds only won twice, and hadn't managed to score more than one goal. There could be no doubting how important the Spaniard was to making the side tick.

I was hosting again today, a Boxing Day family get-together that put my attendance at the game in doubt, until Sky came to the rescue and moved it to an evening kick-off. We started early and booted everyone out at 4pm so I could dash to Elland Road, while my dad shot home to watch on telly, having generously sacrificed his ticket to enable Lewis to attend (who was back from Canada and bailing on his own family get-together). We headed to the Centenary Pavilion to meet a different variation of Woollard as Joe's brother Tom was back from Seville and taking dad Steve's usual place as son Freddie's night-match understudy. With no time for a pre-match pint we settled for a pre-match chat, during which Joe reported that Leeds's rivals had all dropped points against relegation fodder, so victory tonight would restore a ten-point lead.

What followed was a real shock, a role reversal of nearly every other first half we had seen at Elland Road under Marcelo Bielsa. The away team dominated from the off, pressing high and forcing Leeds into mistakes. It took Leeds 20 minutes to finally venture into opposition territory, and when the attack broke down a quick Preston counter ended with the ball in Kiko's net. Leeds struggled to muster a response and it was a relief to get to half-time only 1-0 down. Everyone agreed it had been the worst half of football under Bielsa – sloppy, lethargic, and uninspired – but credit to Preston, they had taken Leeds on at their own game and their bold tactics were paying dividends.

In the second half Preston's tactics were to dive, feign injury, cause skirmishes, and basically waste as much time as possible, but the more annoyed the Leeds fans got, the more the atmosphere built, and the more Leeds got on top. Halfway through the half Bielsa replaced Bamford with Nketiah, drawing a very dishonourable reaction from the Elland Road crowd, the majority booing The Great Man's decision with gusto. Lo and behold his substitution changed the game. Still unable to beat the Preston high press, Leeds now had the option to go over the top, and Nketiah's pace put the visitors firmly on the back foot. For the last 20 minutes normal service was resumed with wave after wave of Leeds attacks, on one flank then the other. Bielsa's full-backs were causing all the danger and Alioski failed to find the equaliser from three great chances, but in the 90th minute Ayling managed to create it when his pull-back to the edge of the box was smashed into the net by Dallas, via a fortunate deflection.

As the players raced back for the restart, the fourth official showed six minutes of added time. Preston were dazed and wobbling, and Leeds went searching for the knockout blow. They nearly landed it in the final moments, Ayling's cross seemed destined to be tapped home by Nketiah until the flying boot of a Preston defender steered the ball to safety and ensured the points were shared. It had been a spirited comeback and pulsating second half, but the performance was far from vintage Bielsaball. Now three games without a win, concern was starting to grow.

Birmingham City 4-5 Leeds United

Leeds's first match of this decade was one of the most spectacular in the club's history, a 1-0 FA Cup victory over their bitter rivals at Old Trafford, when Leeds were a League One club and Manchester United were Premier League champions. But that doesn't even tell half the story, which had started a decade earlier, in October 2000. On the coach back from a 3-0 defeat at Old Trafford, I bet my dad £50 that Leeds wouldn't win there in the next ten years, and in 2008, with Leeds in League One, I accepted an early settlement of £30, the winning amount adjusted after I magnanimously agreed that the spirit of the bet had been compromised by Leeds's fall from grace. I may be magnanimous but I am also half Jewish, so there was no refund when Leeds did the impossible, nine years and three months after the bet was made.

It wasn't just the bet and the victory at Old Trafford that were spectacular; Leeds's performance was too. They took the game by the scruff of the neck from the first minute, playing wonderful football that made a mockery of their league status. The draw that brought the teams together was also spectacular, and was like a cup run itself. Paul and I were watching at our Burke Street bachelor pad, excitement growing as the draw progressed and Manchester United and Leeds remained in the hat. Every ball drawn brought louder and louder cheers, reaching a crescendo when the third-to-last ball left the famous old rivals alone. We were dancing around the living room but Leeds still had to win a replay against Kettering Town at Elland Road, and that game was quite spectacular too. Leeds registered 44 shots but struggled to a 1-1 draw with the non-league side, before an extra-time Mike Grella hat-trick settled the tie. After the spectacular Old Trafford win came the spectacular collapse – a run of three wins in 18 games that almost marred 3 January 2010 forever by costing promotion.

The last match of the decade would also be one of the most spectacular in Leeds's history. The game was live on Sky's Red Button, and with no mates available to watch in town, I dressed Alessandro in his lucky Leeds kit (two games, two wins) and settled to watch it at home. The game got off to a great start when Jack Harrison carried the ball 60 yards upfield to create the opening goal for Costa, then Harrison scored himself to double the lead, via another kind deflection. Having thrown away a three-goal lead so recently, you may have expected a conservative approach from this commanding position, but Bielsaball knows only one way. Leeds continued to steam forward and press high all over the pitch, leading to the next goal when 16-year-old wonderkid Jude Bellingham halved the deficit with the Leeds defence all at sea. Suddenly Birmingham had their tails up and Leeds were on the ropes. I spent the rest of the half waiting for the equaliser, but despite some heavy pressure the lead was still intact at half-time.

I sulked throughout the break, certain Leeds were going to lose. The game had become emotional, Birmingham were a big, physical team and their fans had been whipped into a frenzy; all the ingredients that Bielsa's team sadly couldn't seem to handle. The Great Man dropped Phillips into a back three in an attempt to regain some control, but it didn't work; the match was panning out just as I expected and on the hour it was 2-2, with Birmingham's big centre-forward Lukas Jutkiewicz scrambling home from a corner.

'LEEDS, LEEDS ARE FALLING APART AGAIN!'

Every Championship team's favourite chant rang around St Andrew's. For Leeds fans it feels like kryptonite; you hear it, you believe it. I couldn't see how the players would recover from throwing away another commanding lead, yet at 2-2 they started to control the game again, and ten minutes later Luke Ayling cut inside and unleashed a thunderous strike with the outside of his foot that curled in off the post. It was a stunning goal, so stunning that I was stunned into silence; fortunate really, with Alessandro now asleep in my arms.

The game was getting faster and more frenetic, end-to-end stuff as Leeds pushed to seal the win and Birmingham gave everything for an equaliser, which they scored from an 83rd-minute free kick. It was an awful goal to concede. Leeds's marking was almost as non-existent as their goalkeeper, whose dash into no-man's-land allowed a harmless flick-on to sail freely into the net.

'LEEDS, LEEDS ARE FALLING APART AGAIN!'

I felt sick. I called Frankie in to take Alessandro out of the room. I was far too stressed, and worried for his wellbeing heading into the last five minutes. His departure was well timed as Ayling again powered Leeds forward, playing a clever ball into the box that was beautifully lofted into the top corner by Stuart Dallas. There was no controlling my emotions. I jumped around the living room screaming like a madman. Poor Alessandro wasn't sleeping through this.

'LEEDS, LEEDS ARE FALLING APART AGAIN!'

This time the chant rang out from the away end, but at 4-3 I seriously wondered whether we could still manage to lose 5-4, especially when the fourth official indicated a minimum of six minutes of added time. By now the game had hurtled out of all control and, to my dismay and disbelief, Leeds were still piling forward trying to seal the win. It seems impossible that a team leading 4-3 in injury time away from home could be caught on the counter, but this is Bielsaball and that's exactly what happened. Left-back Gjanni Alioski led a Leeds attack but lost the ball and suddenly Birmingham were attacking with a four-on-three situation. A deep cross evaded the remaining defenders, and the spare man at the back post tucked it away under Casilla for 4-4. Pandemonium.

'LEEDS, LEEDS ARE FALLING APART AGAIN!'

I was crestfallen. 'May as well fold the club,' was my conclusion on WhatsApp, but Leeds weren't done yet. After a 95th-minute Leeds corner was cleared, Gaetano Berardi won a crucial crunching tackle and the ball fell to Costa on the right wing. Costa teased his two markers while Luke Ayling sprinted forward to provide the underlap, then the pass was perfectly timed and perfectly weighted for Ayling to drill low across the six yard box, where Leeds's second-top scorer, Own Goal, nipped in ahead of Harrison and smashed the ball into the net to make it 5-4!

Ayling led the celebrations, dancing uncontrollably in front of the Leeds fans before mimicking Kylian Mbappé's trademark celebration at the corner flag, though perhaps he was actually taking off Trent Alexander-Arnold, Liverpool's incredible right-back, who had impersonated the celebration earlier in the week. It wasn't just the celebration Ayling had copied, but the ability of those two players to drag their team over the winning line. I wondered whether Leeds could still lose 6-5, but thankfully that was beyond even their capabilities and the game finished in a sensational victory, the craziest game of football I have ever seen.

After the match Bielsa joked that he was thankful to be alive (at least I think he was joking), while opposing manager Pep Clotet swallowed his disappointment by proclaiming his love for El Loco, naming him 'the best manager in the country, and maybe the world'. With West Brom beaten at home by struggling Middlesbrough, Leeds continued their run of being top of whichever league they've been in at the turn of the decade, four in a row and counting.

January 2020

1	**Leeds**	**51**
2	West Brom	51
3	Fulham	42
4	Nottingham Forest	41
5	Brentford	40
6	Sheffield Wednesday	39

West Bromwich Albion 1-1 Leeds United

I had now lived through three full decades of Leeds United, and at the start of each the club was on the rise. The 1990s brought the second coming of the club, with Howard Wilkinson delivering promotion and then the title in 1992. At the turn of the millennium Leeds were revived under David O'Leary, with one of the most exciting young teams this country has ever seen, and Simon Grayson ushered in the 2010s with promotion back to the Championship and an imminent return to the Premier League within reach. The middle part of each decade was a different story entirely; a lull in the '90s, calamity in the noughties, and in the 2010s a host of scandalous owners who kept Leeds in the news constantly, despite the club finishing 15th in the Championship every season. For the 2020s I was dreaming big; Marcelo Bielsa delivering Leeds to the real 'Promised Land' and becoming official European champions at last! With El Loco at the helm anything felt possible, but for him to remain at the helm, Leeds had to win promotion this season. No pressure, lads.

For the fifth match running the team in third place had lost, so Leeds and West Brom both headed into the evening kick-off with an eight-point cushion to the play-off zone. There was a late change of plan for me as the pub with Justin was knocked on the head, so instead I headed to my sister's to watch with the family. The match got off to the worst possible start after a corner to West Brom within a minute. I told Lucca about how bad Leeds are at defending corners, but even I was surprised to see how badly this one was defended. Ironically it was a poor corner, and maybe the first error was Costa failing to block it, but instead it looped off his head and West Brom were able to engage in a bit of head-tennis before the ball was hooked towards the top corner. Finally a Leeds player put up some resistance, but Harrison's acrobatic clearance was too little too late as the ball had crossed the line by a few centimetres. Leeds responded well but struggled to cause too many problems for the hosts, who were all too happy to sit on their lead and soak up the pressure.

Eddie Nketiah had finally made his first start at Birmingham and retained his place today, but he was really struggling against two physical centre-backs who hadn't been able to contain Bamford earlier in the season. Injury had restricted Bamford to the Radio Leeds commentary box at St Andrew's, but he was back on the bench tonight, and back on the pitch for the second half. The change worked well and Leeds were soon level when Harrison's great cross was missed by Bamford but Own Goal was on hand to divert it into the far corner; another vital goal for the in-form marksman. Both teams could then have won all three points in injury time. Bamford drilled against the goalkeeper's legs instead of squaring to Klich for an open goal, then Casilla pulled off a great save at the other end and an entertaining game ended in an honourable draw. I was delighted with the point, which kept Leeds's momentum going and kept them top, and I'm always happy when Leeds are top.

Prior to the game, West Brom boss Slaven Bilić had added his name to the ever-growing list of eulogisers over Leeds's great manager, proclaiming it a privilege to manage against Bielsa – 'An unbelievable guy,' as he called the Argentine – and at the final whistle the pair embraced and chatted warmly. It was lovely to see the respect between them, a rarity in football outside of the Bielsa bubble.

But a lovely night was soured when Bielsa confirmed in his post-match interview that Eddie Nketiah would be returning to Arsenal, recalled by his parent club due to a lack of first-team action. El Loco labelled Eddie 'a true gentleman' and praised his professionalism, commitment and ability, but over the next few weeks he would regularly lament Arsenal for recalling him. Leeds had spent good money to get him for the season, and Bielsa had spent a lot of time bringing Nketiah up to speed, only to be stripped of his services just when he had made it into the team.

Despite registering only one victory over the Christmas period, Leeds maintained a fantastic nine-point gap to third. They may have stumbled over it, but another hurdle had been cleared. It was the perfect time for a break from the promotion race and next up was FA Cup third-round weekend. Eddie Nketiah wasn't the only one heading back to Arsenal.

FA Cup Third Round — Arsenal 1-0 Leeds United

There were no blues for me on the first Monday back at work after Christmas as I was heading down to London to see Marcelo Bielsa's first taste of the Premier League. I had been let down once again by the online ticket office, logging in within seconds of tickets going on sale, 'queuing' for 40 minutes, only to find that all 8,000 tickets had gone. Thankfully my Gooner mate, Stoik, was able to get me a ticket in the home end and I was happy with that, content to be an observer for a game I cared little about winning. Although there had been bigger cup ties in recent years (the dizzying heights of the fifth round, no less), this was the first FA Cup tie I'd attended since 2011, when Leeds followed up their 2010 heroics at Old Trafford and White Hart Lane with another great performance and 1-1 draw at Arsenal. In those cup ties Simon Grayson's team made a statement to the rest of the country – the club was alive and kicking. And tonight, live on BBC1, Leeds would send the same message again. This was the grand unveiling of Marcelo's Masterpiece.

I arrived in London just after lunch and checked in to my B&B, which I'd booked on price and location without realising it would be quite such a hellhole. The owner explained they were about to start renovations, but you'd have thought they were preparing for demolition. With no wi-fi I couldn't even do any work, so I headed to the local Wetherspoons via a little walk around the ground, killing time on a bright and pleasant winter's afternoon. When night drew in I took my place in the upper tier of the new Clock End, with Leeds fans directly below and across from me. I must admit I was quite impressed by The Emirates, a stadium I'd declared my hatred for nine years earlier. Maybe the years have softened me, but the view from the top tier was stunning.

Arsenal's new manager, Mikel Arteta, played almost his strongest team. World Cup winner Alex Lacazette partnered £70m Pépé up front, with World Cup winner Mesut Özil behind them. Like Arsenal, Leeds made only four changes, with young Robbie Gotts finally making his debut after being an unused substitute 35 times. El Loco had felt so guilty about this barren run that he called Gotts into his office and told him he'd understand if he wanted to leave Elland Road, but the Harrogate youngster was baffled and going nowhere. Nineteen-year-old goalkeeper Illan Meslier was also making his debut, testing his credentials to replace Kiko, in case the FA banned him for racist language.

Leeds started magnificently. Arsenal just couldn't handle the intensity, with Leeds players snapping at their heels, winning every first ball, and every second ball too. In possession Leeds's passing and movement were exquisite and a joy to behold, especially from the Clock End where I could hear the groans and gawps of the home fans as the Leeds fans cheered their team's every pass. I was beaming with pride. Leeds were humiliating one of the Premier League's 'Big Six', but weren't beating them. At half-time they led the shot count 15-3, with two thirds of the possession, and no goals to show for the domination.

In the second half Arsenal came out fighting and took the lead with a scrappy goal. Despite barely having made a save, it would be wrong to say Meslier's first job was to pick the ball out of his net, as the teenage Frenchman had excelled throughout the first half with his distribution, like a very deep-lying Kalvin Phillips. Once ahead, Arsenal's pace and extra quality began to shine through, while Leeds's intensity waned to the point of alarm. This enabled Meslier to showcase his shot-stopping ability, and the teenager looked as assured with his hands as he was with his feet. It was a great debut that settled a lot of people's nerves about the prospect of losing Kiko. In fact, Meslier looked genuine competition for the number one jersey, regardless of any ban.

At the final whistle everyone was happy; Arsenal were through, and Leeds had portrayed the genius of Bielsa while avoiding the distraction of a cup run or even worse, a replay (apologies to any FA Cup romanticists). The magnificent

Leeds fans lauded their heroes, as did Arteta in his post-match interview: 'Leeds are a great team, a nightmare to play against. Playing them is like going to the dentist.' Back in my hellhole I basked in the glory of Twitter's praise for Bielsa, and went to sleep dreaming of what Leeds might achieve if they managed to finally reach the Premier League.

Leeds United 0-2 Sheffield Wednesday

'Twenty cup finals' tweeted the *Yorkshire Evening Post.* My heart sank. I'd only been awake for 30 seconds and I was already agitated as clearly no lessons had been learned from last season where, to my recollection, the countdown had started at 16. My mood improved at Park Fisheries, and not only because of the lightly battered, succulent fish, and warm bed of fluffy chips beneath. Pablo Hernández was back on the bench, well ahead of schedule, a lovely accompaniment for the best fish and chips in the world. Only a cup of Yorkshire Tea could have squeezed any gains out of today's pre-match feed.

Having been turned around at the coin toss, Leeds got to work on opening the scoring in front of an expectant Kop, but aside from the threat of the in-form Jack Harrison – who almost scored a wonder goal and missed an eight-yard sitter – they lacked any spark. Things got worse in the second half when the players looked physically jaded and Wednesday grew in confidence. Eddie Nketiah might have sparked Leeds into life, but with no striker on the bench I was quite happy to settle for bagels as the game entered its closing stages. Wednesday did have a striker on the bench – the giant Kosovan, Atdhe Nuhiu – and in the 87th minute it was he who set up the crucial first goal. Nuhiu's through ball wasn't the best – it sent his team-mate so wide that the danger seemed to have passed – but a low drive evaded Casilla at his near post and somehow the ball was in the net.

Leeds may have had the time to stage a comeback but they didn't have the energy, and in injury time Nuhiu emphatically fired home the killer blow himself, sending the Wednesday fans into ecstasy. Criticising overzealous celebrations is a pet hate of mine, but the videos of the post-match Wednesday celebrations were completely ridiculous! The victorious players lined up in front of their fans arm in arm, before throwing their shirts into the crowd and taking supporters' scarves in return, singing and dancing like they'd won a cup final. They only stopped short of hoisting Garry Monk into the air. The following week they lost 5-0 at home to Blackburn.

This was a devastating result that had me fearing another inconsistent second half of the season. I knew Leeds were a better team than last season, but the results were the same, so would the ending be the same too? The press weren't helping matters either, and the Radio Leeds post-match interview with Ben White freaked me out almost as much as the defeat. 'What can you say to calm the Leeds fans?' 'Has this squad got enough to finish the job?' 'Do you need signings to reinvigorate the squad?' 'Do the players talk about what happened last season?'

The failure of last season was always going to magnify the pressure this time around, but it infuriated me that the local media would slap it in the players' faces like this, especially in January, with Leeds still sitting six points clear in second place.

Queens Park Rangers 1-0 Leeds United

Marcelo Bielsa's press conferences had never been the same since cherished translator Salim Lamrani went his own way in the summer. Salim was a darling of the Leeds fans, and his parting gift was a series of short write-ups on various players, posted on social media, entitled, 'Memories of Leeds United'. I don't know who came across better in these extracts, the players or Salim himself. This season Bielsa had entrusted his coaches to do the translating, but their English was nowhere near good enough to translate The Great Man's wisdom effectively. Regardless, this week's presser was a must-watch. In a captivating 47 minutes, El Loco fiercely defended Leeds United – from the president right down to the groundsman – amid mounting criticism of performances, results, and lack of transfer activity. One issue he refused to be drawn on was the 'London Curse', a theory that was gaining legs after seven defeats and a draw in their last eight visits to the capital, and one win in 18, saying, 'This is not a geographical issue, I ignore this.'

It took only 20 minutes for the London Curse to strike again. A QPR free kick on the edge of the box was blocked by Ayling, then the ball ricocheted on to the left elbow of Nahki Wells, bounced into the ground and up onto his right elbow, which cushioned it neatly into his path and, with Kiko sprawled on the floor, Wells tapped in to an empty net. You know something is seriously amiss when Bielsa's players appeal furiously, but neither the ref nor the linesman had spotted either handball, so the goal stood. For all Leeds's possession, it took a long Kiko clearance to finally open up QPR, and Bamford cleverly spun his marker and raced through on goal, but harmlessly lofted the bouncing ball well over the bar.

Bamford was a much-talked-about man; a striker who was lauded for his link-up play and work ethic, but who missed glorious chances routinely. With only one senior striker on Leeds's books, many fans believed promotion depended on whether they could sign a front man good enough to replace Bamford. 'At least he's good at penalties,' remarked my brother-in-law, Josh, moments before Bamford was sent tumbling in the box. The referee pointed to the spot and up stepped Bamford, with the Leeds fans behind the goal already singing his name. It was the penalty of a striker devoid of confidence, a feeble effort that the goalkeeper comfortably saved. Bamford stood head in hands, Josh stood corrected. This was not looking good.

The final half-hour was all Leeds, but chronic wastefulness kept the score at 1-0, and then on 87 minutes things went from bad to worse. Kalvin Phillips, who 48 hours earlier was calmness personified when claiming the drop in results was 'no big deal', got himself sent off for a wild and frustrated lunge. Game over. Leeds had lost again, and Phillips's three-match suspension rubbed salt into the wounds.

With one win in seven games, the lead over third place was now down to four points. Incredibly, West Brom also had only one win in seven, so the division's top two propped up the other 22 teams in the form guide; the Championship at its absolute craziest. Confidence was low, spirits were low, and supporters were beside themselves. Since Stuart Dallas made it 4-3 at Birmingham, Leeds fans had watched their players average a shot every six minutes, for six hours, without scoring once. Harder than childbirth, it's no wonder we're deranged.

Leeds United 3-2 Millwall

Normally you want the chance to avenge a defeat at the soonest opportunity, but things had got so bad that a ten-day break was exactly the respite required. And what a great ten days it was. West Brom, Fulham, Brentford and Forest all failed to secure three points from their games in hand, while Leeds secured three new signings. Teenagers Elia Caprile and Ian Poveda were bought for the future, but the one everyone was waiting for was a striker, and after finally admitting defeat in the chase for Che Adams, Leeds signed Jean-Kévin Augustin on loan from Bundesliga leaders RB Leipzig. It was a deal that would cost Leeds £20m to make permanent if promotion was achieved, the biggest transfer in the club's history.

After last season's epic win over Millwall I hoped I'd never see them at Elland Road again, and the dream was kept alive as work dragged me down south. I went for some pub grub with my colleagues and managed to hold off looking at my phone until half-time, when my dad's WhatsApp updates delivered the worst nightmare – Leeds were 2-0 down. Inside five minutes Millwall had scored from a corner (the softest goal my dad had 'ever seen, ever') and the second goal came from a penalty, moments after Millwall had clearly dribbled the ball out of play. The news knocked me for six and I could barely think for the rest of the meal; well, barely think about anything other than the endless torture of supporting Leeds.

Half an hour later I checked my phone again. This time my dad's WhatsApp updates delivered a dream come true – Leeds had pulled it back to 2-2! First Bamford had scored from three inches, then Pablo equalised with a deflected volley. Apparently Leeds were on fire and a winning goal was inevitable, so I sacked my colleagues off, raced back to my room and loaded Sky Go, by which time Bamford had already put Leeds 3-2 up. Bielsa's boys were still piling forward, trying to seal the win, but on 85 minutes Klich blazed a gilt-edged chance over the bar and suddenly it was panic stations again. The last few minutes were horrible, but when Kiko clung on to a high, last-minute corner the job was done, and Leeds were back to winning ways.

For the second season running, good had overcome evil in spectacular style; two stunning 3-2 victories! Maybe Neil Harris was the bogey all along, rather than Millwall. The world suddenly seemed a better place. I was a bit gutted to have missed a classic comeback, but with West Brom dropping more points Leeds were top again, and I'm always happy when Leeds are top.

February 2020

1	**Leeds**	**55**
2	West Brom	53
3	Nottingham Forest	51
4	Fulham	49
5	Brentford	47
6	Bristol City	47

Leeds United 0-1 Wigan Athletic

There was a time when Wigan at home sparked hilarious memories of half-time entertainment gone wrong. Down the years Elland Road has produced decent value at the interval – the time the Kop goaded Peter Ridsdale into giving away a car was always the highlight (just a few short years later the club were giving away pizza – how the mighty had fallen!) – until a new game was piloted against Wigan in 2004.

I can only imagine someone was having a laugh while the health and safety officer was on holiday as the concept was barbaric. A home and away supporter were blindfolded on the halfway line, and the first to run into their respective goal would win. Off the fans went, not in a perfectly straight line. The Wigan fan was lightning quick and, roared on by everyone, he hurtled towards the South Stand, wide of the goal and went crashing over the advertising boards! Sadly, it was back to kicking a ball through a hole after that. Sadder still, Good Friday 2019 had overshadowed the memory forever.

Despite this season's results practically being an exact replica of last season, nobody was predicting a repeat of Wigan's miracle victory at Elland Road. It was their only away win of last season, a result that saved them from relegation, and this season the Latics were in the relegation dogfight again, with only one away win. This was the perfect chance for Leeds to register consecutive victories for the first time in two months, but I didn't wear my lucky socks and I didn't put up any resistance when my dad requested double-fish. It was a slap in the face of the Football Gods, yet I was too confident to fear their wrath; lightning doesn't strike twice.

As usual, Leeds took complete control after a few minutes of jostling, and Jack Harrison was again the main threat. He was unlucky to hit the post after leaving two defenders on their arses in the penalty box, and from the next attack he miscued from five yards with the goal at his mercy. Harrison wasn't the only one struggling in front of goal and, despite his match-winning brace on Tuesday, Patrick Bamford's confidence appeared to have reached new lows. At the end of the first half his shot from the centre of the box resembled a frantic defender's wild clearance, then at the start of the second half, his free header at the back post resembled a calm defender safely conceding a corner.

Cometh the hour, Wigan won a corner. Cometh the inevitable. As always, Pablo Hernández was positioned as a one-man wall to prevent a low delivery, and the corner cannoned off his shoulder and looped towards the Leeds goal. Surrounded by players, Kiko Casilla could only flap a fist in the general direction of the ball, which continued unabated into the far corner of the net. Elland Road was aghast. For the next half-hour Leeds toiled, but Wigan knew exactly what to do; defend the box with ten players and feign injury at every opportunity. Neither Leeds nor the referee were going to punish these tactics, and as the clock ticked down the result became so inevitable that complaining about the lack of injury time, or a possible penalty for a clear handball, was pointless. In the dying seconds came one last chance when Bamford finally got his finish right, but his header was cleared off the line, then Hélder Costa got the rebound all wrong, blasting the ball high into the exasperated Kop. Lightning had struck twice.

I was demoralised walking back to the car. After the Sheffield Wednesday defeat I was worrying about slipping into the play-off spots; now I was worrying about slipping out of them. Was it possible that Leeds could crumble entirely? Much of the post-match talk surrounded the exclusion of new striker Jean-Kévin Augustin, with the fans furious that Augustin hadn't even been named on the bench as an option to throw on regardless of whether he was Bielsa-ready. The criticism was harsh considering Bielsa had thrown on a fully fit striker in Tyler Roberts, but the overreaction of the supporters reflected our desperation for promotion, and the panic that it seemed to be slipping away.

Nottingham Forest 2-0 Leeds United

I thought we had seen the peak of Bielsa's press conferences before the QPR defeat, but we had seen nothing yet. For the pre-Forest presser El Loco came armed with notes, answered just five questions in an hour, and was seething throughout; eyeballing the journalists, waving his arms, even raising his voice. The main bone of contention was Jean-Kévin Augustin, with Bielsa explaining for 20 minutes why he was not on the bench against Wigan, and that it was disrespectful to Leeds United to expect anyone to walk into the club and straight into the team. So when Augustin was named on the bench for the Forest match, it was a surprise, a relief, and a boost.

It was a Saturday evening kick-off and, fearing the worst, I decided it would be best viewed in the pub, where I could drink my sorrows away. I regretted the plan within seconds of walking in to The Alex as it was heaving with rugby fans and all the main screens were showing the Calcutta Cup match between England and Scotland. I was supposed to meet Towse and Kinky Dave, but it was so busy we ended up watching the game tucked away in opposite corners of the pub, with neither party willing to risk losing their limited vantage point.

Leeds started brightly until yet another calamitous goal knocked the stuffing out of them. The defence parted like the Red Sea – Ayling was too eager to win the ball back, White was caught napping and Cooper was ten yards behind the defensive line, but all that was forgotten as Kiko Casilla shamefully dived out of the way of Ameobi's near-post drive. It was another terrible piece of goalkeeping, and the tenth game running that Casilla had conceded from the first or second shot at his goal, inspiring me to nickname him The Cat Flap.

The rugby finished and the Tarquins cleared off as the second half commenced. We may have had a better view but it was a hands-over-the-eyes performance. Leeds dominated possession without ever looking like scoring, although the Forest goalkeeper was called upon once, clawing Cooper's header off the goal line in tantalising fashion. With 20 minutes to go El Loco introduced Augustin but he barely got a sniff, and in the last minute of injury time, with the rest of the Leeds players in attack, Jack Harrison was caught in possession on the halfway line and Forest raced through to seal the win.

Leeds remained second, ahead of Forest only on goal difference, when just eight weeks earlier they had held a 14-point lead in the live table. Next up was a trip to Griffin

Park, a ground Leeds hadn't won at in 70 years, to face the London Curse and a Brentford team who were now within striking distance themselves.

The beers had done nothing to soften the blow of defeat. I was gutted. My post-match kebab did help for the two minutes it took to scoff, but then it was back to the reality of walking home in the pouring rain, reflecting on a run of two wins in ten games, and wondering why the Football Gods can't give Leeds United a goddamn break, just for one season.

Brentford 1-1 Leeds United

By Tuesday morning I was starting to feel a bit better. Leeds were second in the table and had dominated every team, so I knew they could still get promoted, but I had completely written off tonight's match. In my head tonight would be rock bottom and the season would start again on Saturday. Already at peace with the defeat, I headed over to my sister's house feeling relaxed for a change.

Nearly all Leeds fans were calling for wholesale changes; some with reason, some without. Calling for Poveda to start without ever having seen him play was silly, but asking for Augustin was more understandable, as were claims for the freshness of Shackleton, Berardi, and/or Roberts. Hoping The Cat Flap would be dropped was unanimous, but there was no surprise that the only change was the return of Kalvin Phillips, and with Phillips at his Rolls-Royce best, Leeds were back to their normal selves. Brentford couldn't get a foothold in the game as the visitors dominated possession, but once again they missed chances to take the lead, and once again all their good work was undone by a horrendous goalkeeping error. Kiko sank to laugh-or-cry levels, allowing Cooper's back pass to run under his foot, then stumbling to the floor in his desperation to reclaim possession, leaving Saïd Benrahma with a tap-in.

Nobody was blaming the London Curse for this calamity, this was all on Kiko, but it was impossible not to feel sorry for him.

The Leeds players redoubled their efforts and were rewarded with an equaliser when Brentford's keeper made a blooper of his own, dropping Harrison's corner at the feet of Cooper, who stabbed the ball into the top corner. Lucca jumped around the living room, but I remained calm, still programmed to expect the worst. The worst never came, and never looked like coming. Like the first half, the second half was all Leeds, but half-chances for Bamford, Costa and Harrison came and went without testing the keeper, Augustin came and went without testing the keeper, and at the other end, thankfully, there was no testing of The Cat Flap. So the game ended in a draw that kept Leeds above Brentford, and still in second thanks to the law of physics that says whoever beats Bielsa must lose their next game. Forest manager Sabri Lamouchi had tried to cheat science by making wholesale changes to his team, but still they were beaten 1-0 at home by relegation-threatened Charlton.

It was another winless game, but to most Leeds fans it felt like a watershed moment. Was the wobble over? After the defeat at Forest, Luke Ayling had given a haunting interview with the weight of the world clearly on his shoulders, looking and sounding totally drained and utterly dejected. Just three days later Leeds looked completely rejuvenated, even in the face of more goalkeeping adversity. It was later revealed that The Great Man had cancelled the usual post-match debrief of the Forest game and instead he delivered a long and stirring speech reaffirming his belief in the players. It didn't half do the trick.

Leeds United 1-0 Bristol City

Leeds were clinging on to second place by their fingernails and the chasing pack had closed in so tightly that today's seventh-placed opponents could overtake them with a 7-0 win. Forest's draw at West Brom in the early kick-off prevented Leeds from dropping to third ahead of kick-off, and secured their place in the top six for another week, no matter how many goals Bristol put through The Cat Flap. For family reasons I made a last-minute decision to sacrifice my attendance at the game, a decision taken as a good husband and made easier by our excellent record in games I've missed. My dad was left to battle Storm Dennis on his own.

From the very first minute Leeds bombarded their opponents and three chances were missed in the first two minutes before they continued to tear through Bristol almost at will. Leeds 'finally' broke the deadlock after 15 minutes, but it was a goal that did little to improve their efficiency figures; the goalmouth scramble featured four mishit shots before Ayling forced the ball into the net with the fifth bite of the cherry. Ayling had been a firm fans' favourite from the day he arrived at Elland Road in August 2016, plucked from the scrapheap at Bristol City for a few hundred grand after Lee Johnson deemed him not good enough for the Championship. There was no doubting where his loyalties lay, but he grabbed his Leeds badge and celebrated in front of his former supporters for good measure.

The domination continued throughout and Leeds reached new heights in chances created and new lows in chances missed. Even the new superstar substitute striker got in on the act, Augustin screwing wide when he really should have opened his account and settled the match. My dad thought it was the best Leeds had played under Bielsa, but without a second goal it was nerve-wracking right up until the final whistle put Bristol out of their misery.

Following up the positive result at Brentford was imperative, so this was a massive three points for Leeds, and a morale-boosting clean sheet for the defence. The cake was iced with the points dropped by all of Leeds's rivals and they had breathing space again with a three-point lead over Fulham in third. The terrible struggles in front of goal still caused me great concern, but if one goal is enough to win then you take it every week.

Leeds United 1-0 Reading

Kiko Casilla's racism hearing finally took place in the week leading up to this game. His defence was heavily reliant on high-profile character references, so the process took a full week to complete. While the FA deliberated over the evidence he remained available for selection but, considering it was his word vs two Charlton players, this was widely expected to be his last game for some time.

A bitterly cold wind blew through Elland Road for the second game running and, attacking the Kop, Leeds looked to blow their opponents away. However, the wind was taken out of their sails when Kalvin Phillips hobbled off the pitch injured, and although Ben White deputised competently, the Kop were unable to suck the ball into the net. Responsibility would fall on the South Stand in the second half, and thanks to The SS5 Movement they were more than capable. This was a plan devised by a small but boisterous group of 100 or so fans in 2013, intent on adding atmosphere to the derelict end of the ground. It soon spread to a full stand of exuberance, like an away end for the home fans; an awesome feature of Elland Road.

It took just over ten minutes for the South Stand to do their job, ably assisted by the genius of Pablo Hernández. Pablo had struggled for form since returning from injury, prompting people to question whether age had finally caught up with him, but El Mago put any doubters in their place when pouncing on a loose ball in the box. With a flick of his instep Hernández jinked inside the defender, and with a flick of his outstep he sent the ball flying into the top corner of the net. The noise was deafening, the relief palpable, and the 'limbs' in the South Stand a thing of beauty.

Leeds remained in control for the rest of the game, but as the finish line approached the fear of a sucker-punch grew. Reading hadn't created a single chance, but in the last minute of injury time 35,000 Yorkshire hearts were in mouths as Reading's big centre-back spun Leeds's big centre-back and bore down on Casilla. The under-fire keeper rushed out and smothered the shot, and when the rebound was blasted high over the bar the crowd let out an almighty roar, followed by raucous chanting for Kiko. The Kop took an age to return the ball, partly to waste time but also to prolong the homage to a goalkeeper who had been through the wringer on and off the pitch. Kiko stood patiently by the advertising boards until a fan emerged with the ball and handed it over while delivering a little pep talk before player and fan shared warm pats on the back in a lovely moment.

At the final whistle there was more adulation for Casilla. In a very public and deliberate show of affection, Marcelo Bielsa marched on to the Elland Road pitch for the first time to congratulate his match-winning goalkeeper; maintaining an emotional distance from his players serves to amplify moments like these. Now all eyes were on the big screen, and for the second week running all of Leeds's rivals had slipped up and the gap was increased to five points. Elland Road was overjoyed; Leeds were back on track.

Middlesbrough 0-1 Leeds United

Having fled the country last season, I decided to face my fear and return to The Riverside, a stadium I hadn't seen Leeds win at since 2001. I was hopeful it would be third time lucky in the home end with Tom, and as we supped our pre-match pints in the concourse the TVs showed highlights of my last visit to Boro, a 3-0 thrashing that included a hat-trick from none other than Patrick Bamford. 'Put a bet on Bamford to score in the first five minutes,' instructed a little old lady to her husband, her pessimism backing up the doom and gloom of Tom and Sillsy during our pre-match chicken parmo (when in Rome 'n that). They expected Leeds to devour Boro like I devoured my Parmo, but I assured them it would be a painful night for all of us because, like Tom and Sillsy eating a Parmo, Leeds just can't finish.

After a brief surge in form over Christmas, Middlesbrough were back in grave relegation trouble and Jonathan Woodgate had received the dreaded vote of confidence from the board. But there was no confidence from the fans. The Riverside was so quiet and sombre and within minutes of kick-off it was clear to see why, as Middlesbrough instantly looked clueless and hopeless. Without the injured Yorkshire Pirlo, Leeds didn't look a great deal better and Bamford missed a golden chance to win the little old lady her bet, but for the rest of the half they struggled to click into gear. Things finally clicked in injury time, Mateusz Klich calmly finishing in-off the same post Hernández had struck seconds before. I was mostly surrounded by red seats but kept my composure out of respect for my host, although inside I was jumping for joy.

With only one goal in the game I was a quivering wreck throughout the second half. Opportunities to seal the win went begging, and Bamford progressed from failing to score goals to preventing them when he inadvertently blocked Ayling's deflected cutback on the goal line. In the end Leeds were fortunate not to be punished for their inefficiency as Boro's one clear chance crashed off the top of the bar, then in the 89th minute the incompetence of the referee came to their rescue when a free kick was blocked in the box by the outstretched arm of Stuart Dallas. The ref was staring straight at it, but having denied Leeds stonewall penalties in each half he decided to let bygones be bygones.

As we debriefed on the way to the car it was clear that Tom and I were experiencing polar opposite emotions. Tom was devastated and left contemplating League One, with Neil Warnock the only man who could save them, while I was elated and dreaming of the Premier League, the Football Gods the only ones who could deny us.

Hull City 0-4 Leeds United

After waiting five months to hold the hearing, and spending over a week deliberating, the FA waited until 7.30pm on Friday (before a Saturday lunchtime kick-off) to deliver the verdict on Kiko Casilla's racism charge. The timing of the verdict seemed vindictive, but the decision and sentence was accepted by club and fans; Casilla was found guilty and banned for eight games. Leeds would be without their highest earner – a 33-year-old three-time Champions League winner with the best clean sheet record in the division – for one of the most important periods in the club's history. Into his shoes would step a 19-year-old rookie, plucked from the reserves of a French second division team when Bailey Peacock-Farrell left for Burnley. Yet despite Illan Meslier's inexperience, most fans were hopeful this could become a blessing in disguise. Kiko had channelled his inner Bowyer and found top form since the hearing started, but you could never be sure what he was going to do next.

It's no cliché that there are no easy games in the Championship, and week in and week out the bottom teams beat the top teams, but if ever there was going to be an easy three points then this was surely it. Hull were bottom of the form table and winless since New Year's Day, had sold their two best players in January and had 11 first-team injuries. Nevertheless, this was the day my promotion-race sleep deprivation kicked in. I was awake from 1.30am, pondering the match, Kiko's ban, the points Leeds had thrown away and the points on offer in the matches to come. When it was finally time for the game, Alessandro donned his new Leeds kit and we settled on the sofa; me quietly confident, Alessandro anything but quiet.

It's also no cliché that when you're near the bottom of the league everything goes against you, and with barely five minutes on the clock a wicked deflection diverted Ayling's long-range drive unstoppably into the net. A few minutes later Hernández's 20-yard shot crashed off the inside of post and bar, but for the rest of the half Leeds were well below par. Fortunately their opponents were even worse than Middlesbrough and never troubled the young debutant in goal.

In the second half Leeds scored within minutes of the kick-off again, and at 2-0 the game descended into shooting practice for the visitors. The points were sealed beyond any doubt with probably the best counterattack of the season so far. It started by Leeds's corner flag where three white shirts suffocated a Hull attack, winning the ball back and playing some beautiful football to work their way out of a tight space. The move flowed upfield into the Hull half where Roberts fed Costa on the right, Costa switched to Klich on the left, and with the Hull defence bamboozled, Klich laid it on a plate for Roberts to sweep the ball into the net. 'We want four' chanted the Leeds fans, and moments later Roberts scored again with a brilliant diving header. A penny for the thoughts of substituted Patrick Bamford, who had scored two goals in 1,000 minutes while his replacement had two goals in five minutes! Bamford then had to listen to the Leeds fans singing his song, with one slight tweak of the lyrics: 'Du, du, du, du... Tyler Roberts!'

With four goals, and a clean sheet for Meslier, it had been the perfect start to the weekend.

Another thing I love about Bielsa's philosophy is his desire for players to take risks, which gives them the freedom and confidence to reach their maximum potential, and is not limited to outfield players. In his post-match analysis of Meslier's performance The Great Man highlighted his 'risk-taking' as a major attribute. Yes, El Loco even wants the teenage debutant in goal to take risks. He truly is one of a kind!

March 2020

1	West Brom	69
2	**Leeds**	**68**
3	Fulham	63
4	Nottingham Forest	60
5	Brentford	57
6	Preston	56

Leeds United 2-0 Huddersfield Town

It's not entirely fair to call the West Yorkshire derby a one-sided rivalry, but it tells a tale that Huddersfield playfully call it 'El Flat-Capio', whereas the Leeds fans mock the fixture's importance with the chant, 'You mean fuck all to us.' Before relegation from the Premier League in 2004 the fixture rarely saw the light of day as Huddersfield bounced around the lower leagues while Leeds bounced around Europe, and during this period I attended many Huddersfield games with Billy and his mate, Edwyn (when I wasn't watching Leeds). I've celebrated on the McAlpine pitch, celebrated on the terraces at York, celebrated promotion at the Millennium Stadium; I was always celebrating when watching Huddersfield, so much so that I became a good-luck charm to Billy and Edwyn (I must add these were hollow celebrations, I was just along for the craic!).

When Leeds dropped all the way down to League One in 2007, El Flat-Capio returned, and some feisty matches built the closest thing Leeds have had to a local rivalry. Sadly, I remained a good-luck charm for the Terriers and with me in attendance two rip-roaring 2-2 draws in the 2010 promotion season were as good as it got, sandwiched by four home defeats and an away loss. I was in Vegas when Town were thrashed 4-0 on their long-awaited return to Elland Road, and I was working when they were thrashed 5-1 the day after Brian McDermott's phantom sacking. The only time I have ever seen Huddersfield Town lose was when Neil Redfearn's team of Cellino misfits beat them 3-0 at Elland Road in 2014.

Derby day started with a happy accident as the 12.03pm train was cancelled, but the previous train was running late and I managed to hop on just in time. I updated Billy who dashed to the next stop and also hopped on just in time, thus we were in The Hop supping Yorkshire Blondes with Edwyn 15 minutes ahead of schedule. Joe Woollard soon joined us and the beers and merriment flowed, maybe even overflowed as Edwyn decided we should have Jägerbombs with our pints. Well, it was their cup final after all, and me and Joe were thrilled that Fulham had been held to a draw in the early kick-off. The pre-match booze-up left us short on time and we decided to keep things in our own hands by walking to the ground. We reached Bremner Square at 3pm, where we said our goodbyes and I told Edwyn to hurry up or he'd miss Leeds's first goal. It was almost a year to the day since a pre-match booze-up led me to miss Pablo Hernández's goal of the season vs West Brom, and incredibly history repeated itself.

This time I made it in to the ground, but was just walking up the Kop stairs when Luke Ayling flew through the air to meet Harrison's deep cross with a flying volley that crashed in off the bar. The build-up play had been mesmerising too, and it was a goal you could watch over and over again. It was no fluke either, as footage emerged after the game of Ayling crashing home a deep Harrison cross in training the day before, an almost identical goal, minus the celebration that was instantly iconic; the release of the topknot, the knee slide, and the air guitar. While players, substitutes, coaches, and fans went potty, Marcelo Bielsa sat totally deadpan on his bucket, staring at the ground and sipping coffee. He'd seen it all before.

The rest of the half was men against boys, as it had been almost all season, and early in the second period Patrick Bamford broke his latest duck with a beautiful, nonchalant dink into the net from all of one yard. Elland Road was buoyant, as was their team, and Jack Harrison almost rivalled Ayling for goal of the season but, having jinked passed three defenders, his 20-yard curler smacked the upright. Thereafter, Huddersfield managed to take the sting out of the game without ever looking like getting back into it, so Illan Meslier celebrated his 20th birthday with a clean sheet on his home debut and Leeds celebrated a fifth successive victory, plus a return to the top of the league as West Brom slipped up again.

I was now as confident as I had been all season that Leeds were going up. Fulham seemed to be the only realistic threat, and they were seven points behind and due to visit Elland Road in ten days' time. Naturally, Bielsa urged for calm in his post-match presser, pointing to the 11-point lead that had been lost earlier in the season, yet the mood of the Leeds fans was better reflected by the words of Huddersfield manager, and president of the Marcelo Bielsa Fan Club, Danny Cowley. He had praised El Loco as a football pioneer earlier in the season and went to greater lengths today: 'I enjoyed that in a sadistic way. Leeds are the best team in the league by a mile, Bielsa is a genius, I'm looking forward to seeing how the Premier League teams cope with them next season.'

Covid 19-0 Leeds United

There had long been jokes about a meteor strike or nuclear war ending the world just when Leeds United are about to win promotion back to the Premier League, but over the last 16 years it never came to that. The team always managed to mess things up themselves. However, now that Marcelo Bielsa had seemingly beaten everything that could be thrown at him, the Football Gods enlisted the help of the big man upstairs, who delivered a global pandemic like no other in living memory. Covid-19 originated in China at the end of 2019 and by late February it was ripping through Europe, causing havoc in the sporting calendar as many countries banned mass gatherings.

They say a week is a long time in football, and that's certainly the case during a pandemic. The coronavirus got little airtime before or after the Huddersfield match, but less than a week later – fittingly on Friday, 13 March – it was announced that the UK was suspending all football in a bid to slow down the spread of infection. By the end of the following weekend the whole world was in lockdown, and in England people were only allowed to leave their homes for essential groceries, pharmacy visits, and once per day for exercise. Only essential workplaces remained open, and everything else, including schools, was closed.

Under Andrea Radrizzani's ownership Leeds United are a class act, and the club led the way in their response to the shutdown. Immediately it was announced that all players and coaching staff would be taking huge wage deferrals to enable the non-football staff to continue to receive full payment. In contrast, many super-rich Premier League clubs initially took advantage of the government's furlough scheme, before eventually backtracking for PR purposes.

Exercise equipment was already on standby and promptly delivered to the players' homes so they could continue personalised training programs, and Leeds even had their own in-house Covid testing process. Marcelo Bielsa was determined that nobody would be better prepared than his team when football returned. If football returned.

Lockdown

April

The first month of lockdown wasn't too painful. My friends and family were all well and I continued to work from home as normal. I couldn't play football on a Thursday night, or squash on a Monday, but I preserved my sanity by trying to get 'Bielsa-fit', learning to juggle, and embarking on a 20-year dynasty with KRC Genk on *Football Manager*. There were some pleasant aspects of life in lockdown too. The break from the 100mph 21st-century lifestyle was refreshing, as was a whole month without any football of any kind, anywhere (except in Belarus, where the government advised that vodka and saunas were all that was needed to beat Covid-19).

The chasm left by football was filled with speculation and debate about when, if and how it would return in this country. The leagues in France, Belgium, and Scotland were all cancelled, as were the lower leagues of English football. Some settled their season on points per game, and some null and voided altogether, with no promotion and no relegation – music to the ears of the struggling Premier League clubs who shamelessly campaigned for this drastic approach. When it became apparent that the Premier League clubs would have to refund broadcasters to the tune of £760m if the season was curtailed, suddenly everyone was okay with completing the fixtures, though the relegation-threatened clubs still tried to argue that relegation should be scrapped regardless.

With the Premier League, UEFA, and the EFL all adamant that the 2019/20 season would be completed when safe to do so, tentative plans were made to resume fixtures in mid-June, almost certainly behind closed doors. Having a potential restart date was a great boost, but the prospect of Leeds finally securing promotion to the Premier League with not a soul in attendance was galling.

Norman Hunter and Trevor Cherry RIP

On 17 April, Covid tragically claimed the life of one of Leeds United's greatest legends. Norman Hunter was a star of the great Don Revie team that put Leeds on the map, making an incredible 726 appearances, playing over 50 games in nine consecutive seasons (in the tenth he 'only' played 49), and being the only player to appear in all 12 cup finals of the era. He was also the recipient of the inaugural PFA Player of the Year award in 1974 and, last but not least, a World Cup winner with England. What a career.

Norman epitomised the spirit of Revie's Leeds side, his nickname 'Bites Yer Legs' striking fear into all and sundry, but my generation knew him better as the co-commentator on Radio Leeds, a job he did for over a decade. We'd grown up listening to him analyse defeat after defeat (that bloody radio curse), and in many ways his words taught us what it meant to be Leeds.

When Norman finally succumbed to coronavirus it was a terribly sad day. I was pushed to tears by a fan's photo on Twitter, taken during a stadium tour on the morning of a recent game, of Norman stood on the touchline looking out over the Elland Road pitch. There he will always remain, in spirit and in name, as the South Stand was renamed the Norman Hunter Stand in the coming days.

Tragically, the Leeds United family lost another legend less than two weeks later. Trevor Cherry made over 400 appearances for the club, having joined Revie's squad in the early '70s, and famously marked the great Johan Cruyff out of both legs of the European Cup semi-final victory over Barcelona. Cherry succeeded Billy Bremner as captain, and also led England, another wonderful footballer and a great man.

In 1973 Revie labelled his Leeds team 'the most consistent team that ever lived.' That remains true to this day, and will probably remain true for all time. Between 1965 and 1975 they challenged for the top honours every season, nearly winning trebles in most, with a team that barely changed throughout the decade. This is where the Revie team is unique, with almost a full squad of one-club men, mates who grew up together and excelled for a generation. Because of this, they are all deeply attached to the club, and though my generation isn't lucky enough to have seen them play, we are fortunate to have grown up with these legends in and around Elland Road, and to have heard all the stories first-hand. Leeds United will never forget them, but when they are gone we will miss them so much.

May

In the second month of lockdown things started to get tough. Every Saturday was another day when we could have been celebrating promotion, culminating in the last day of the season on Saturday, 2 May. This would have been Marcelo Bielsa's 100th match in charge and should have been the crowning glory of his incredible reign, one of the best and most emotional days of my life, a day of thanks and praise for the sacrifices he and his squad had made, the redemption for the last 16 years; the highlight of a lifetime supporting Leeds.

By now it was clear that if the season were to conclude then the last nine matches would be played out with no fans in attendance, which made me wonder whether I wanted the season to finish at all. I'd spent 16 years waiting to celebrate returning to the Premier League, finding solace each passing year with the idea that the longer we waited the greater the emotions would be when the moment finally came.

If the season resumed that moment could be stolen from us forever. But if the season was scrapped perhaps Bielsa would leave? Phillips certainly would, other players too, and the club's financial position would be dire. And the thought of the last nine months counting for absolutely nothing was horrible. Eventually I convinced myself that Leeds had to achieve promotion however it came, and any other thought was selfish. Everyone at Leeds United deserved Premier League football, they deserved to achieve their goal.

So it came as a relief when the EFL finally confirmed that promotion and relegation would stand in all divisions, even if the season couldn't finish, in which case the table would be decided by 'unweighted points per game'. This meant that if another ball wasn't kicked, Leeds would be crowned champions and promoted to the Premier League, with a PPG figure of 1.919. Having been formed in 1919, this would be quite the coincidence in the centenary season! Nobody had more to lose if the season restarted, but Leeds voted against deciding the season on PPG. Everyone at the club wanted to complete the job on the pitch, especially Bielsa and his players, who were desperate to atone for last season, and desperate to prove they had the bottle to finish the job.

By the end of May the Premier League had announced its return date, and the EFL soon followed suit. The promotion push would recommence on 21 June.

Marcelo Bielsa vs Rocco Dean

It was a normal Monday morning, working from home as usual. Just before noon, Frankie came to my office to alert me that there was a strange man in a hat knocking at the door. 'Do you know anyone who drives a blue Golf?' I didn't, and told Frankie to ignore it, before coming to my senses and deciding to 'deal with it' myself. On my way to the front door I glanced out of the window, 'Oh my god, it's Bielsa!'

Only two people had read *Marcelo Bielsa vs Leeds United*, my account of El Loco's first season at Leeds. My dad was one of them and implored me to send a copy to The Great Man.

The coronavirus outbreak had opened a door as football was postponed and everyone was in isolation; in theory Bielsa might have time on his hands to actually read it.

So I decided to take the plunge. I messaged a postman I know, apologising for sounding like a five-year-old and asking if a letter addressed to 'Marcelo Bielsa, Wetherby' would reach its target. He was confident it would. Already armed with an A4 envelope and first-class stamps, I was able to post the 'book' without the embarrassment of going to the Post Office, and I included a cover letter in Google-translated Spanish:

> *Marcelo,*
>
> *Thank you for reviving Leeds United, and building a new culture for the 21st century. You are a true inspiration, we are very lucky to have you in Leeds. With free time maybe you can learn English, maybe my book can help! At least it will be a memento of your unforgettable first season in England. I spent time writing it because it meant so much to me and I never want to forget it (even if the ending was painful). Also,*

I wanted my baby (Alessandro Marcelo) to know the sensational story of a club reborn.

Stay safe during these worrying times,

Rocco

I posted the book with my address on the back of the envelope as a 'return to sender', feeling hopeful that Bielsa, a man of the people, would acknowledge receipt of the book (if it ever made it to him). Nevertheless, I was at least half joking when asking Frankie, 'Anything from Bielsa?' whenever the post arrived over the next few days.

Thinking back to the moment I saw Bielsa on my driveway is like recalling a dream. It doesn't make any sense, but in the moment it did. I don't think I was even that surprised. There was no double take, I knew it was him and just needed to get to the door. I was unwashed and unkempt, wearing last night's T-shirt, trackie bottoms, and a bush of hair on my head and face, but none of that crossed my mind as I opened the door to The Great Man and his driver, aka the 'strange man in a hat' (perhaps this was the 'spy' from the Spygate fiasco).

'Hello!' My delight was surely beaming through.

'Hello, I received this letter, did you send this to me?'

Bielsa pointed to the envelope I posted, which his driver was holding.

'I did, Marcelo, yes.'

'Thank you for your work, it is very good, I want to thank you with these presents.'

Bielsa handed me a see-through plastic bag from the club shop. Inside was a dark grey Leeds United centenary away shirt, and pinned to the bag was a little badge; El Loco's face with the crests of Leeds and Athletic Bilbao in the background, and a Spanish strapline later translated as 'In the crazy (loco)

Once a blue, always a white

Better to have loved and lost, hey dad

We go again

Ten-man who?

Boathouse beers

Never felt closer to God

Yorkshire Pirlo, centenary hero

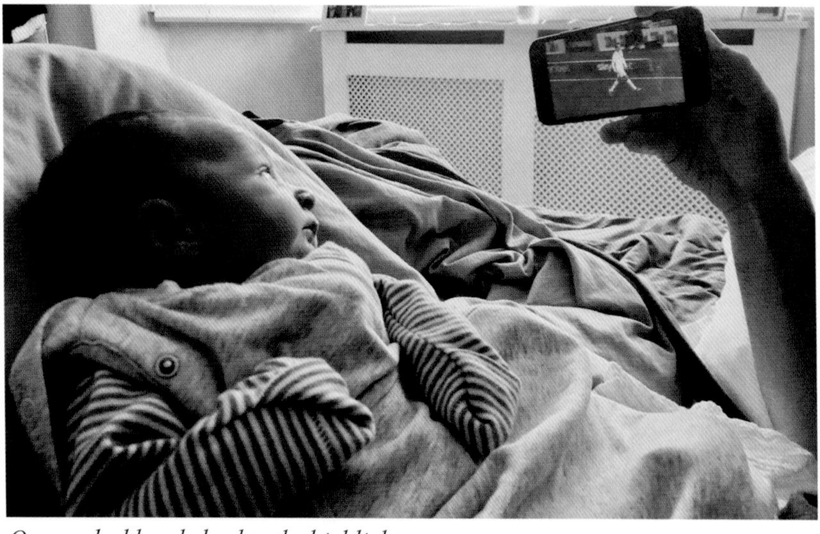

One week old and glued to the highlights

The last bastion of English football

Leeds United Christmas do

3-0, game over…

The national unveiling of Marcelo's masterpiece

A grey day above and below the magnificent new East Stand

The customary lap of honour

Leeds, united

El Flatcapio: a friendly derby

Look at what you could have won

The last goal of the old normal

A gift from God

Alessandro in the Kop

The new normal: the patio end

The end of the exile

Promotion party

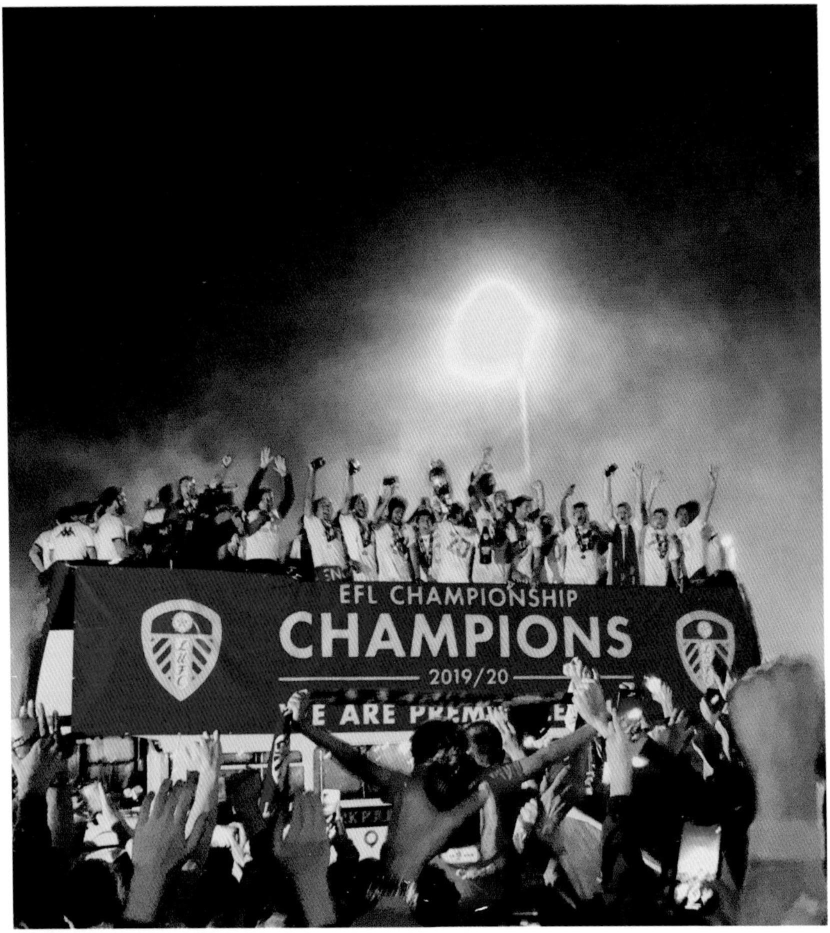

Leeds United, Football League champions again

'We are all so much older now, 16 painful years...'

'...A man was just a boy when he cried those relegation tears.'

way, one lives better.' Bielsa made a point of pointing that out to me, and gave a little bow of respect.

'Thank you, Marcelo, thank you so much, you are a wonderful man. Can you understand the book?'

'Yes, he understands.'

Bielsa nodded in agreement with his driver's answer and as I sensed we were in the final throws of the encounter, my next move was critical. Marcelo Bielsa is at your front door, so what do you do? What do you ask him? Invite him in? Ask him to bless Alessandro?

'Can we do a photo?!'

Cringe. I wanted a memento of the occasion, but this remains a regret, especially considering the reply.

'Sorry, I don't like photos.'

It is widely acknowledged that Bielsa never turns down photo requests, but that was in the Old Normal, and I certainly wasn't going to argue with The Great Man.

'No problem, that's absolutely fine, I understand!'

With that, and another round of thank yous, Marcelo and his driver headed back to their car, while two builders working on our neighbour's house gazed on in amazement.

It's fair to say I struggled to do any work for the rest of the afternoon, and even Frankie was shaking with excitement. When trying on my Leeds top I saw it had '22 HARRISON' on the back. I was at a loss why he had given me Harrison's shirt, until I read *The Quality of Madness*, a biography on Bielsa's career by Tim Reach, which explained how the number 22 in Argentine betting phraseology is known as 'El Loco'. The attention to detail boggles my mind, in the same way my mind boggled at the realisation that Bielsa had been sufficiently moved by my 'work' that he felt the need to thank me in person. Receiving these gifts in the post would have still been an amazing gesture. It also struck me that the shirt was a 'UK Small'. I am not a small man, but I had chosen this size in my previous purchases from the club shop. Surely a large or medium would have been the safe bet. Could his meticulous nature have driven him to check my order history?!

I barely slept for the rest of the week, unable to stop replaying the episode on loop in my head, analysing my performance and searching for any missing information. And counting my lucky stars; Marcelo Bielsa was in our neighbourhood, on my doorstep, thanking me! What a man he is.

June 2020

1	**Leeds**	**71**
2	West Brom	70
3	Fulham	64
4	Brentford	60
5	Nottingham Forest	60
6	Preston	56

Cardiff City 2-0 Leeds United

After a 100-day absence football was back, but while most people rejoiced my feelings were mixed. I was looking forward to watching Leeds play again, but the fact we would not be there to witness the run-in was still eating away at me. Phil Hay wrote an article on The Athletic in the lead-up to the match, listing all the failures and calamities Leeds fans have experienced in the 16 years since relegation from the Premier League. It was supposed to be a motivational piece and everyone in the comments section was foaming at the mouth for Leeds to finally end the story arc, yet it only served to emphasise my belief that Don Revie was right all along about the Gypsy Curse. 'And nobody will be there to see or celebrate the redemption, possibly the most diabolical of all the listed incidents.' My comment received no 'likes' but Phil did comment that he understood how unfair it is, bless him.

My enthusiasm for football was significantly boosted when Fulham, Leeds's closest rivals outside the top two, lost 2-0 at home to Brentford in the Saturday lunchtime kick-off. A few hours later, West Brom had been held to a goalless draw by Birmingham, and Forest in fifth and Preston in sixth had both failed to win too. Without kicking a ball, Leeds were the big winners of the day.

It also helped that their first game behind closed doors was at Cardiff City, a place I'd happily never go to again, having experienced two of my darkest footballing memories there. My first visit to the Welsh capital came in January 2002, when Leeds were top of the Premier League but were knocked out of the FA Cup by third-tier Cardiff. I'd always wondered what football was like in the 1980s, and I experienced it that day at a riotous Ninian Park, which proved to be the day the metaphoric *Titanic* crashed. Unbeknown to us fans, Leeds had been heading straight for the iceberg for some time and after defeat in Cardiff the team capitulated, sinking from the top of the Premier League to the bottom of League One in just five years. Along the way a rescue boat passed by unexpectedly, in the form of the 2006 Championship play-off final. A dour team with a dour manager headed down to Cardiff's Millennium Stadium and I went with them, enduring what was probably the most depressing afternoon of my life. The rescue boat sailed away with David Healy and Robbie Blake sat watching from the decks, Captain Blackwell scandalously failing to deploy two of his best players as Leeds were thrashed 3-0 by a dour team with a dour manager.

The Championship has come a long way since Kevin Blackwell and Aidy Boothroyd faced off in the most underwhelming 'Master vs Pupil Showdown' of all time. The football dinosaurs no longer rule the division; today it is led by cultured teams with cultured managers, but the dinosaurs are not yet extinct and Leeds would come up against one today in Neil bloody Harris. His team's epic comeback at Elland Road had sparked a collapse in form that saw an 11-point lead disappear, yet heading into the return game Leeds had the chance to extend the gap back to ten points, like nothing had happened in the six months between.

What transpired does not require any in-depth description. It was the same as nearly every other defeat Leeds had suffered under Marcelo Bielsa. The team had 70 per cent possession but could have played all day, maybe all week, without scoring. The chances created were mostly blasted off target, the ones that weren't brought heroic saves from an inspired goalkeeper, and even when the keeper was beaten, Patrick Bamford was on hand to clear off the line. Yes, for the second time this season the beleaguered striker prevented a goal. There was nothing Pat could have done, he just couldn't get out of the way in time. Some mothers do have 'em!

At that point Cardiff hadn't had a touch of the ball inside Leeds's box, yet were leading 1-0, all part of Harris's masterplan no doubt. Junior Hoilett had pounced on Kalvin Phillips's first mistake of the season and smashed the ball into the Leeds net, then in the second half Liam Cooper's first mistake of the season led to Cardiff's second and final shot on target, which flew in off the post. Defeat had seemed inevitable the moment Bamford blocked Harrison's equaliser, and by full time I was over it. Leeds still had a seven-point lead on third and there was one fewer game to play, no need to panic. The lads had a full week to lick their wounds and prepare for the run-in, with eight games in 25 days to decide their fate, starting with the biggest of the lot, Fulham at Elland Road.

Leeds United 3-0 Fulham

After the luxury of not having to fret over the promotion race for three months, my angst and paranoia returned with a bang in the lead-up to a pivotal weekend in the Championship. The top four were facing off, and I was convinced Leeds would lose to Fulham, then crumble under the pressure as their rivals closed in. It's never blind pessimism with me and in my head the evidence was overwhelming.

The most concerning rival was Brentford, who had the best attack, the best goal difference, and a fully fit Pontus Jansson returning to their defence. A Friday night victory over West Brom moved Brentford into third, just five points behind Leeds, and on Saturday, their West London rivals arrived at Elland Road looking to cut the gap to four points. Last season my deepest fears all came to fruition, but this would be an afternoon where my fears were all turned on their head.

My main concern was the difference in each team's number nine. Fulham had Aleksandar Mitrović, the Championship's top scorer with a conversion rate double that of Leeds's Patrick Bamford. Yet it was a torrid afternoon for Mitrović, whose main contribution to the game was a second-minute elbow, violent and deliberate into the face of Ben White. The officials missed it but the young centre-back shrugged it off in ice-cool fashion, a reaction that must have unnerved Mitrovic the way he'd hoped to unnerve his victim. The big Serb's performance deteriorated throughout the game, while White grew in stature and ultimately walked off as the man of the match. Not only did Mitrović draw a blank, Bamford atoned for his Cardiff calamity by opening the scoring after ten minutes. It was a clinical finish, aided by the great wing play of Hélder Costa and great awareness of Tyler Roberts, who taught Bamford a lesson in how to get out of the way of a goalbound shot.

Another concern of mine was the newly introduced drinks breaks halfway through each half. I felt this would aid our opponents, giving them a breather from the relentless Leeds pressure and interrupting the home side's rhythm. Yet I found myself yearning for the drinks break as Fulham took complete control after Bamford's goal. In total contrast to the rest of Bielsa's reign, Leeds ended the half having seen only 35 per cent of the ball, but 1-0 ahead having converted their only chance. Was this the 'new normal' that the Government kept banging on about? Despite Leeds's half-time advantage – and unrelated to Chris's theory – I was now even more convinced they were going to lose. My dad was worried too: 'It's like a bad dream. Can Bielsa sort it out?' My two-word response won't have calmed his fears: 'He can't.'

Oh how I underestimated The Great Man! Despite conjuring up the goal, off went Bamford and Costa and on came Alioski and Pablo Hernández, whose expected absence had been the smoking gun for my case of doom, as without Pablo Leeds's win percentage literally halves. With Pablo, Leeds instantly looked a different team, doubling their lead ten minutes after his introduction. This season Leeds had scored more goals from defending corners than they had from our attacking corners, and they were at it again today, setting a new PB of 11 seconds to move from box to box, and only three kicks of the football. From Meslier's quick throw, Ayling passed first time up to Klich, the Pole swept a beautiful ball down the right wing to the rampaging Harrison and Harrison squared it to Roberts who, along with four Fulham defenders, ran past the ball in comedy fashion as it kindly rolled into the path of Gjanni Alioski. In the old normal the madcap Macedonian would have lashed it on to the M62, but today he calmly placed the ball into the bottom corner of the net, before blowing celebratory kisses to the cardboard cutouts in the Kop.

With a 2-0 lead the swagger returned. Leeds were back to their best and Fulham looked spent, but they still needed another goal before I could relax. Step forward Pablo Hernández, who arched a majestic 60-yard through ball into the path of Jack Harrison, who outpaced and outmuscled the defender before poking the ball through the keeper's legs and into the net. I cracked open a celebratory beer, sat back, and actually enjoyed the last ten minutes of the match. This new normal lark wasn't so bad after all.

Everyone agreed that Marcelo's half-time masterclass won this match, and fittingly it was The Great Man who delivered the final slap to my fickle, pessimistic face. As with the introduction of drinks breaks, I was concerned the new rule allowing five substitutions would be yet another way for opponents to waste valuable time, but on this most curious of days the new rule played in Leeds's favour again. El Loco took the opportunity to withdraw Hernández, wrapping the little Spaniard in cotton wool for the last few minutes as his work was done.

Leeds had taken a huge step towards promotion. I was relieved and delighted, yet I still couldn't shake the feeling of regret as Alioski embarked upon a lap of honour, applauding the 15,000 cardboard cutouts that packed the lower sections of the ground. As it happens, a work trip to America would have meant me missing this game even if Covid-19 hadn't disrupted the season, but that offered no real consolation, nor did the theory that Leeds may not have been so composed in front of goal with 35,000 fans holding their breath. Strangely, I did find comfort knowing that Alessandro's image was in there somewhere, his first appearance at Elland Road, on a day that felt like the beginning of the end of the Premier League exile.

Leeds United 1-1 Luton Town

It would have been poetic if this had been the first game with 'Crowdies', exactly 340 months since my first appearance at Elland Road against the same opponents. For Alessandro, Luton would be his second game; perhaps Leeds will entertain

Luton at my grandson's third game. Talking of sequences, there was a striking symmetry to the run-in; three weekend trips to teams pushing for the play-offs, and four midweek home games against teams fighting relegation.

Having watched the two previous games alone in trepidation, I decided that a problem shared is a problem quartered and invited Justin, Fan, and Nige round to my patio (lockdown regulations banned them from coming into the house). Considering our inept first-half performance against Fulham and the difference Pablo's introduction made, I suspected Costa would make way for El Mago, or perhaps Klich's incredible run of 87 consecutive starts would come to an end. I even wondered whether Bielsa might finally drop Bamford. 'You know Bielsa,' was my dad's response when I posed the question to him. He certainly did, the team was unchanged.

The 11 that struggled against the most expensive squad in the division also struggled against the cheapest. Despite 'enjoying' almost 80 per cent possession, Leeds only managed two shots in the first 45 minutes, and corner after corner after corner. Those corners had me pulling my hair out as the worst of the lot landed near the halfway line, and the rest never cleared the first man. At half-time, LUTV's expert summariser, Ben Parker, had some interesting advice for The Godfather of Modern Football: 'He needs to tell them to play better.' Perhaps Ben's simplistic approach would have done the trick, but El Loco was thinking outside the box. Having lost Cooper to injury early in the game, the ever-ruthless Bielsa withdrew his replacement, Gaetano Berardi, and switched to a flat back one. The plan backfired when the one defender, Ben White, allowed Luton's danger man, Harry Cornick, to dribble into the penalty box, and curl a magnificent finish into Meslier's top corner. One shot, one goal.

Straight on to the pitch came Pablo Hernández, and ten minutes later he started the move that brought the equaliser, Stuart Dallas with the calm finish after Alioski calmly picked him out of a crowded penalty box. Social distancing briefly went out the window as the Patio End erupted and three points were within reach. Much like the game at Luton, chances came thicker and faster as the clock ticked down, but much like the rest of the season Leeds just couldn't put the ball in the net. Despite leading the division in 'Big Chances Missed' (with a whopping 27 according to the statisticians), Patrick Bamford managed to break new ground when Jack Harrison's wizardly wing play put a chance on a plate for him. Six yards out, with the goal at his mercy, Bamford inexplicably let the ball sail past him and out for a goal kick. I was dumbfounded.

Leeds continued to bombard the visitors and in the 96th minute came a carbon-copy chance; this time it was Alioski with a sumptuous cross, plumb on the head of Costa. In the middle of the box with not a defender in sight, the marquee signing imitated last season's marquee signing and did absolutely nothing as the ball simply bounced off the top of his head and rolled out towards the corner flag. Another bewildering effort. His team-mates let out wails of despair; the Patio End went ballistic.

It transpired that both Costa and Bamford blamed the floodlights for their sins. Having never known the West Stand floodlights to distract anyone before, I find it hard to believe that it suddenly it happened twice in one game, but then again, I've never seen two misses quite like these. Perhaps it was the work of the Football Gods.

I can only imagine the scene inside a full Elland Road when Costa missed that header; the anger, the frustration, the disbelief, all amplified by the chances previously missed, the enormity of the two points dropped, and the last 16 years of trouble and strife. I would have loved to experience that moment and the emotions swirling around the Kop, which need to be shared with 35,000, not three.

July 2020

1	**Leeds**	**75**
2	West Brom	74
3	Brentford	69
4	Nottingham Forest	67
5	Fulham	67
6	Cardiff City	61

Blackburn Rovers 1-3 Leeds United

This one really hurt. In a parallel universe, me, Justin and Fan would have finished work early on Friday and headed across the Pennines to meet Bartle's Barmy Army in the Darwen End. The match was scheduled for the 20th anniversary of the murders of Chris Loftus and Kevin Speight, and 8,000 Leeds fans would have turned their backs on the first minute of play as they had in Istanbul, in protest at the inhumane response to the deaths of our fans from everyone not associated with Leeds United. The atmosphere would have been supercharged and the memory would have lasted a lifetime.

In the new normal, George was visiting from London and we headed over to Nige's to watch the match on LUTV. The three of us had been together at Ewood Park in April 2004 when Leeds beat Blackburn 2-1 in a crucial relegation six-pointer. The victory came during a period of resurgence, and at the final whistle we sang in total belief, 'Leeds are stopping up!' Sixteen years later, we were still waiting to celebrate another Premier League victory. In the aftermath of floodlight-gate the players held a team meeting to clear the air, clearly more concerned about their performances since lockdown than the league table itself, which had barely changed. Bielsa was unmoved, but injuries forced him into changing his team. The left flank was freshened up, with Alioski and Douglas replacing Costa and Dallas, and Jack Harrison was given fresh impetus by switching to the right. This would be the first game Costa and Dallas had missed this season, leaving Klich, Harrison, and White as the last of the ever-presents; quite a contrast to last season, when the team was ravaged every week.

A refreshed Leeds looked much more like their pre-lockdown selves, but nevertheless their 2-0 half-time lead was heavily reliant on the upside-down laws of the new normal. A confident, clinical, cool, calm, and collected Patrick Bamford gave Leeds an early lead, from a chance that came about when the referee failed to spot Klich barging over the Blackburn player in order to steal possession in midfield. It wasn't just the referee who was on Leeds's side; so too was Lady Luck. Within minutes of the goal, Sam Gallagher screwed inches wide when clean through, then Lewis Holtby smashed the inside of the post from ten yards. Harrison collected the rebound and was tackled while trying to dribble his way out of danger, the tackle sent the ball flying into the Leeds net but the ref disallowed the goal because a finger had been laid on Harrison.

Only 13 minutes were on the clock and I already felt like I couldn't take much more. My anxiety was quelled somewhat by the first direct free kick Leeds had scored in a quarter of a decade, a 30-yarder from Kalvin Phillips, curled so sublimely into the top corner that it was almost worth the 30-month wait. Jermaine Beckford, doing the co-commentary on LUTV, was so shocked he even praised 'the build-up play'.

Early in the second half Blackburn scored a free kick of their own, but there was barely time to panic as five minutes later Klich's weak effort squirmed through the butterfingers of the keeper to restore the two-goal cushion. Leeds saw the game out in a professional manner, happily aided by the referee who, despite six substitutions, two goals, and a drinks break, only played two minutes of added time.

While Leeds were beginning their exile from the Premier League in August 2004, George and I were working in Cheltenham following flooding in the area. We missed the opening-day victory at home to Derby but were able to sneak off to watch Leeds lose at Gillingham and draw at Wolves. During a trip back to Yorkshire to replenish our equipment, we were able to take in a home draw against Forest, but every other waking hour of Leeds's first month of Championship football was spent hauling sodden carpets out of Gloucestershire homes. One customer gave us a bottle of wine for our (heroic) efforts, and that bottle had sat proudly on my desk ever since. Daring to dream that this was Leeds's last month of Championship football, I took the bottle to Nige's, and at the final whistle George and I finally cracked it open in celebration. Unfortunately, this was white wine and it aged worse than Wayne Rooney, so the fruits of our labour were mostly poured down the drain.

Leeds United 5-0 Stoke City

As they did last season, Sky decreed that Leeds should play after their rivals in every game up until the last day of the season. If they were to fall apart again, nobody would blame the fixture schedule (nobody did last season), but clearly this was not an even playing field. Leeds would have to play their last five fixtures in just 13 days, though of more concern was the psychological turmoil of watching your rivals chasing you down, one by one. First up on Tuesday evening were Fulham, who ended Forest's faint hopes of automatic promotion with a 1-0 win at the City Ground, reducing the gap to five points. Kicking off an hour later were Brentford, and at half-time they trailed 1-0 to relegation-threatened Charlton, but two goals in the last 15 minutes cut the gap down to three points. On Wednesday it was West Brom's turn as they beat a lacklustre Derby team to regain top spot. By teatime on Thursday, all eyes were on Leeds.

The 2019/20 season had followed the patterns of 2018/19 almost identically: a great start, an indifferent autumn, a pre-Christmas seven-game winning run, a post-Christmas collapse, and a spring rebirth, culminating in an alarmingly familiar situation. Heading into the Easter weekend last season Leeds needed ten points to be sure of promotion, and heading into this fixture – originally scheduled for Good Friday – they needed ten points to be sure of promotion. On Good Friday last season, Leeds hosted a Wigan side who knew a win would probably be enough to escape relegation; this time they hosted a Stoke side who knew a win would probably be enough to escape relegation. All season the Leeds players insisted they'd learnt from their mistakes of last season and now was the chance to prove it.

The team news was hotly anticipated this evening, and The Great Man responded by breaking the first commandment of management: 'Thou shalt not change a winning team.' Costa and Dallas were recalled in place of Douglas and Alioski, Bielsa probably deducing that a team that was winning a league was a better bet than one that had won a match. Leeds started brightly, and before long came the customary jaw-dropping miss when Tyler Roberts, six yards out with a seemingly open goal, saw his shot miraculously blocked on the line, though not by Bamford, I'm pleased to report. Leeds were dominating, so I was quite content heading towards half-time bagels, but with the last attack Hélder Costa was recklessly fouled just inside the box and the ref awarded the penalty. Mateusz Klich assumed responsibility – his 50 per cent conversion rate from the spot was shamefully the best in the squad – and the Pole calmly rolled the ball into the net.

Leeds doubled the lead as close to half-time as they'd taken it, and this was a goal touched by the genius of Bielsa. The recalled Dallas split the defence for the recalled Costa, who had enough time to perform a pointless pirouette before poking past the keeper.

Lewis rang from Canada and we spent the rest of the game on the phone as goal after goal flew into the Stoke net. Pablo Hernández had been introduced at half-time and was at his mesmeric best, enabling Leeds to run riot. Cooper smashed in the third from Pablo's pull-back after the evergreen Spaniard's inspired off-the-ball run across the penalty box, weaving through eight Stoke players in order to pop up in space on the right, having taken a short corner from the left. Pablo then scored the fourth himself with a 20-yard finish, out of the top drawer and into the bottom corner, after Bamford's clever dummy and a 30-pass move; Bielsaball at its finest. In stoppage time Bamford was rewarded for a great performance with his 16th goal of the season, smacking Ayling's scorching 70-yard through ball in off both posts. The players had been true to their word, emphatically proving that they had indeed learnt from last season. They did to Stoke exactly what they should have done to ten-man Wigan.

I went to bed in a state of bewilderment. I kept looking at the scoreline, but it wouldn't sink in, no matter how many times I looked. 5-0! I woke up at 2.45am and soon it was clear

I'd not be getting any more sleep, I was far too excited. I spent the next four hours rewatching footage of the goals, reading through Twitter's analysis, and wondering whether Pablo's run across the box was truly his own genius, or some whacky short-corner routine. That seems far-fetched even for El Loco. This was purely the work of El Mago, his greatest magic trick yet. 'Pablo is so good he can improve me as a coach.' I finally understood the words Bielsa had spoken just a month into his reign.

Swansea City 0-1 Leeds United

The day before Leeds took on Swansea came the news that the club had lost yet another legend, Jack Charlton. Despite being a one-club player, Big Jack wasn't just a Leeds United legend, he was a true football great. Even more than his incredible achievements in the game – winning every domestic trophy for Leeds, the club's record appearance maker, Football Writers' Player of the Year, an astonishing 96 goals from centre-back, and a World Cup winner with England – it was Jack's personality that elevated him to such levels that the outpour of emotion was nationwide, almost worldwide, and a minute's silence was held at all matches across the country. They really don't make them like Jack anymore; a wonderful man who enjoyed a wonderful life, and who enriched the name of Leeds United.

With four games left the fixture list had thrown up a cracking round of matches as the four teams fighting for the automatic promotion spots came up against four teams fighting for the last play-off spot. Fulham were first up again, beating Cardiff on Friday night, before Brentford kept up their perfect post-lockdown record with victory at Derby. The teams chasing Leeds had clocked up 14 wins in a row between them, but on Saturday afternoon West Brom flinched, stuttering to a 1-1 draw at Blackburn, which kept Leeds top of the league by one goal. What a boost. With a win at Swansea, Bielsa's boys would not only move to the brink of promotion, they would take control of the title race. Win at Swansea? Leeds hadn't done that since 1964, the day Don Revie's rising stars – with Jack Charlton at the heart of defence – sealed promotion to the top flight. Were the stars aligning?

Surprisingly there were no pre-game nerves for me as I was excited and expecting a cracking match. It was a beautiful summer's day, and El Patio Marcelo Bielsa was at full capacity (six people, as dictated by the government's covid guidelines). The first half failed to live up to the billing and was a dour affair between two teams who looked happy to play out a draw. That may have been befitting of the situation – Swansea needed a point to leap into the last play-off spot, Leeds needed a point to stay top – but it was not in keeping with Bielsa's philosophy. El Loco called upon El Mago at half-time.

After the break the men in charcoal and pink cranked up the intensity, seemingly suddenly aware of the opportunity in front of them. Swansea remained happy to contain and frustrate, hoping their two strikers, Rhian Brewster and André Ayew, would catch Leeds off guard at some point. It wasn't going to happen as Cooper and White were impeccable at the back, and young goalkeeper Illan Meslier was outstanding behind them, calmness personified. Midway through the half, Pablo's superb 40-yard ball was volleyed perfectly across goal by Harrison into the path of Patrick Bamford. Bamford had half the goal to aim at with his six-yard header, but directed the ball back towards the scrambling keeper who pushed it to safety. Having previously been quite content with a point, I was now desperate for a winning goal, desperate for Pat's miss to be filed under comedy and not tragedy.

Step forward, yet again, Pablo Hernández. With time almost up, Leeds won the ball on their own byline and Phillips passed across the six-yard box to Ayling, who set off up the wing. In the 90th minute of the 43rd match of the longest season ever, Ayling didn't let up after passing infield to Klich; instead he bombed on, covering the length of the pitch in 13 seconds to latch on to Costa's pass on the Swansea byline. With six Leeds shirts in the box, Ayling chose to pick out Hernández. It's an indescribable feeling, the realisation your team might be about to score, and as the ball fell to Pablo on the penalty spot my heart skipped a beat. 'GO ON!' This wasn't an instruction but a shriek of desperation, a plea for Pablo to put it in the net. After a touch to set himself, Pablo hurriedly stroked the ball towards the corner. 'GO-ARN?!' This second noise was less a plea for the ball to go in, more a question of whether it would. The ball rolled past the outstretched arm of the keeper, bounced off the post, and into the centre of the net. 'YEEEEEAAAAAHHH!!!!' Our cheers reverberated around the neighbourhood, Leeds had done it, Pablo had done it, it just had to be Pablo! The final whistle sparked a second wave of celebrations as Leeds were on the brink of promotion. Surely this was their year, surely!

After the game I was back on Alessandro duties, but by 9pm he and Frankie were tucked up in bed and I was able to bask in the glory of Pablo's goal, and Bryn Law's commentary, over and over again. 'Out wide it goes to Hélder Costa, there's space. And there's an overlapping run from Ayling and Ayling gets the ball. And there are men in the box. And it comes for Pablo Hernández. And Pablo Hernández… SCORES A GOAL FOR LEEDS UNITED! OOOAAAHHH! GOAL-A-GOAL-A-GOOOAAAAL! HERNÁNDEEZZ!' Maybe it lacked the finesse of John Helm's famous commentary from 30 years earlier, when Gordon Strachan fired in a last-minute winner to send Leeds to the brink of promotion ('Have you ever seen a better goal? And have you ever seen one better timed?'), but Bryn's words brought tears to my eyes, especially when someone added the customary backdrop of the *Titanic* music!

Watching the replays, it dawned on me that the Leeds substitutes all went as potty as if they'd scored the goal themselves, while the players on the pitch were too knackered to join the joyous huddle by the corner flag. This was a poignant portrait of The Bielsa Effect – everyone giving everything for the cause.

Leeds United 1-0 Barnsley

In the third-to-last game of the 1989/90 promotion season, struggling Barnsley came to Elland Road and beat Leeds 2-1. 'A game that should have come with a health warning,' declared the *Yorkshire Post* the next day. In chilling similarity, struggling Barnsley came to Elland Road in the third-to-last game of the 2019/20 season. Nobody at Leeds needed reminding that the job wasn't done yet, but it would have been nice to get that health warning.

'I might come to the promotion party myself,' said poor Frankie, who couldn't wait for it all to be over. She worked out that, having been with me for eight years, she'd 'lived through' half of Leeds's 16-year exile. No doubt she has suffered like I have; ruined weekends, ruined birthdays, ruined holidays, and the perpetual fear of Leeds losing and how it would impact my mood. With Leeds so close to promotion I was struggling to sleep and struggling to eat. I hadn't slept past 4am since the Stoke game, and after every meal I felt sick, which I put down to my new fitness regime and a shrunken stomach, but Frankie was convinced it was Leeds-related anxiety (she would be proved right). Knowing that things would only get worse, I booked the last ten days of the season off work. Ten days of partying were on the cards if results went Leeds's way in game week 44.

Game week 44 of 46, yet none of the 24 Championship teams knew for definite which division they'd be playing in next season. Proof, if it was needed, that the Championship really is the most competitive league in the world. Furthermore, nine of the 12 midweek fixtures were genuine six-pointers between teams both fighting against relegation, both fighting for a play-off spot, or both fighting for automatic promotion. The most competitive league in the world, yes, but that didn't stop it producing one of the least competitive games I've ever known, Wigan racing into a 7-0 half-time lead in a relegation six-pointer against Hull (disappointingly, it only finished 8-0). More importantly, Fulham and West Brom played out a dire 0-0 draw that kept Leeds top and ended Fulham's chances of overtaking the whites. The next day Brentford beat Preston to extend their admirable winning run to eight games. They were now only one point behind West Brom and three behind Leeds, with a superior goal difference to both.

Thursday was a long day, though another early kick-off – 5pm, as had become standard in the new normal – was a saving grace. I headed over to Rick's house to watch it with him and Terry, although this was never going to be a party, just a means to an end. Bottom-of-the-table Barnsley came out fighting, pressed high and didn't let the league leaders settle. They had already breached Leeds's defence once when a corner brought another clear chance, but thankfully the free header flashed wide of the post. Seconds later Leeds went in front as that man again, Own Goal, was in the right place at the right time to turn Bamford's cross into the net. It wasn't as spectacular as the Brian Gayle own goal that won Leeds the First Division title in 1992, but it would prove just as significant.

Leeds reached half-time a goal to the good, but neither the introduction of Pablo Hernández nor Bielsa's tactical tinkering could stem the tide of the game, and Barnsley were dominant.

Chances came and went as the visitors defied the logic of the table with their performance, while justifying it with their terrible finishing. It was horrible to watch. The Leeds players seemed paralysed by the magnitude of the situation they were in, while El Loco seemed to throw his philosophy in the bin, bringing on all his defenders as Leeds packed their own box rather than the opposition's.

Terror-stricken, there was no chance of seeing out the win in style, but the boys had the grit, determination, and the experience to hold firm, and when the final whistle blew they celebrated like a team that had achieved their goal. Screams of joy and relief from Dallas and Cooper, tearful hugs between Berardi and White, Phillips smiling from ear to ear. The players were well aware, these three points may just be enough.

Huddersfield Town 2-1 West Bromwich Albion

I was of course delighted with the Barnsley result, but the match itself was so dreadful and nerve-wracking that I couldn't take any enjoyment from it. In a packed Elland Road there would have been wild unforgettable celebrations, but behind closed doors we got all the stress and none of the joy. Nevertheless, promotion was as close as it could possibly be, and for Leeds to be denied, both West Brom and Brentford would need to win their last two games, and Bielsa's team would need to lose both of theirs. Like most Leeds fans, I am psychologically damaged to such an extent that I still felt sick with nerves, but on the morning after the Barnsley match the anxiety was coupled with excitement. This could be the day Leeds United return to the Premier League.

In the penultimate game of the 1998/99 season, David O'Leary's swashbuckling young Leeds side beat Arsenal 1-0 at Elland Road to effectively win the title for Manchester United. Leeds repeated the trick in the penultimate game of 2002/03 when victory at Highbury secured their Premier League status for another year, but secured another title for their enemies in the process. Now the boot was on the other foot as Huddersfield were taking on West Brom and needed a result to secure their Championship status, and if they got it Leeds were up. I arranged to watch the game with Huddersfield Bill, but he cancelled at the last minute so I headed to the pub on my own. By the time I arrived, scanned my phone, filled in the required information for 'track and trace', and listened to all the rules and regulations of being in the pub, Huddersfield were already 1-0 up. By the time my shandy arrived it was half-time, and 1-1. Leeds were 45 minutes from promotion and I was getting nervous.

The second half was all West Brom, but despite their dominance they were toothless in attack and suddenly Leeds were only five minutes from glory. Then came the moment. A Huddersfield counterattack, a great ball in to Emile Smith Rowe, a great first touch, and a left-footed finish past the flat-footed keeper, into the corner of the net. The goal sparked thunderous roars of delight from the loner in the corner drinking shandy. It was the goal that sent Leeds United to the Premier League, and it was scored at 7.19pm, or on the 24-hour clock, 19:19, the year the club was founded. The stars had aligned!

The reason I was on shandy was to keep my options open, and despite pleas from the club to stay at home I just had to go to Elland Road. I had expected a hundred or so people to be gathered on Bremner Square, but as I approached the ground the traffic was similar to a matchday. I ditched the car in a car park and rushed down Elland Road to be greeted by a fabulous scene. Through blue and yellow smoke, thousands of Leeds fans were waving flags, swinging scarves, bouncing, cheering, chanting, and rejoicing. Now it really sank in, and I needed a deep breath to control my emotions. After worrying for months, not only about securing promotion but also that we would not be able to celebrate it at all, this was a joy to behold like few others in my life.

As dusk fell over Elland Road things took a wonderful turn. Unbeknown to the fans, the Leeds players had arranged to watch the Huddersfield game together and were all in the East Stand celebrating. Once they were spotted through the top-floor windows, it wasn't long before our heroes emerged from the lower concourse to rapturous cheers from the elated supporters. Kalvin Phillips played cheerleader in an hour-long sing-song, while players and fans booted footballs to each other, back and forth over the locked East Stand gates. When the players waved goodbye to continue their celebrations inside the stadium, I called it a night and drove home as high as a kite. The rest of the fans stayed and partied into the early hours, before returning to the ground in the morning to clear up their litter. The Bielsa Effect runs deep.

So how did Marcelo Bielsa celebrate our promotion? One may have expected him to enjoy the moment in quiet serenity, reflecting on his achievement over a nice bottle of Malbec while ploughing through videos of the next opponents. The reality was quite the opposite, and thanks to social media we were able to see the beauty in all its glory. First came the video of El Loco emerging from his humble bedsit in Wetherby, greeting a flock of adoring fans with clenched fists, waves, thank yous, photos with the kids, and a wagged finger at the gentleman who told him he was God. 'We love you, Marcelo!' The cries somehow felt even more genuine coming from mothers and grandmothers. From there Bielsa headed to Elland Road, where he snuck in through the West Stand and walked across the pitch to join the party in the East Stand as his players chanted, 'MAAARCELO BIELSA,

MAAARCELO BIELSA!' There was a long, emotional hug for Pablo, a man who had dedicated the end of his career to achieving this goal, a genius who had dragged Leeds over the line. There was an excited hug and a kiss on the cheek for Kalvin Phillips, the linchpin of his team. 'Kalvin Carajo! The best! The best!' But my favourite video was when The Great Man spotted Pat Bamford, and greeted him with arms outstretched and a beaming smile, 'PATRIIIICK!' Bielsa had put his neck on the line for Bamford, and Bamford had borne the full weight of that support all season. The suffering was over, the job was done.

The next day I woke up at 4am and spent the whole morning watching footage of the promotion party and Sky Sports News bulletins about Leeds's return to the Premier League. Then on *Football Focus* came perhaps the most emotional footage of all, a poem read by Nikolaj Coster-Waldau, aka Jaime Lannister on *Game of Thrones*, the most famous of Leeds's many Scandinavian supporters. The poem was a pseudo voicemail left for Bielsa, which perfectly summed up our feelings about promotion and El Loco, and signed off with a sentence that wells me up just writing it, because it comes right from the heart: 'We love you, Marcelo, more than you'll ever know.'

At lunchtime, Brentford faced Stoke. Suddenly the Bees had promotion in their own hands and needed only a draw to overtake West Brom, but only a win would keep the title race alive. Looking for a ninth straight victory, Brentford folded under the pressure and lost 1-0, sealing the Championship title for Leeds United. A part of me was disappointed that they weren't able to secure the title on the pitch, but the rest of me was delighted. Leeds had won the Championship! One day after the 16-year wait for Premier League football ended, Marcelo Bielsa's 16-year wait for a trophy was over. Bueno.

Derby County 1-3 Leeds United

Thursday; win critical match. Friday; win promotion. Saturday; win the title. Sunday really should have been a day of rest. Instead, with heavy heads and bleary eyes, the players headed to Pride Park to face their greatest Championship foes, while the fans staged a big party in Leeds's Millennium Square. We gave Leeds a miss and held our own champions party in Paddy's garden. It was a euphoric feeling watching Leeds in beautiful serenity as the result was irrelevant, there were no more permutations, we could just sit back and bask in the glory of Marcelo Bielsa's champions, and a guard of honour that was steeped in karma. Since that play-off semi-final win at Elland Road at the end of the previous season, the Derby players had lost the final, lost their manager and seen their captain sacked. Now they would line up and clap those defeated and broken-hearted Leeds players on to the pitch as champions. What a twist of fate!

Straight from kick-off Leeds were relaxed and dominant, while the fans on Paddy's patio chatted, laughed, and drank merrily. At half-time it was 0-0 and everyone was happy. In the second half Derby took the lead, but two minutes later Pablo left Wayne Rooney in his wake to pick up a loose ball and curl home the equaliser. Soon Leeds were ahead when a brilliant team move was finished off by Jamie Shackleton, his first professional goal, then a few minutes later the win was sealed by Own Goal, now Leeds's third-highest scorer. Leeds may have fielded a team of drunks but their performance was befitting of champions, and after the match the whole squad celebrated on the Pride Park pitch with champagne, flags, and flares. The scenes were wonderful, players and staff milking it for all its worth. Victor Orta even brought out the binoculars for good measure, in a swipe at Derby for their Spygate-mocking celebrations last May.

Later that evening came the sobering news that Gaetano Berardi had torn his ACL in the first half, an injury that would rule him out for the whole of the next season. Berardi was 31 years old and his contract had expired, yet while most out-of-contract players protected their own interests and refused to play for their clubs post-lockdown, Bera had been determined to help Leeds finish the job. I was devastated for the lionhearted heartthrob, though the pictures of him on crutches in the celebrations would serve as a timeless reminder; Gaetano Berardi was a true warrior, and a wonderful servant to the club, who put side before self, every time.

Leeds United 4-0 Charlton Athletic

So to the last fixture of Leeds's 16-year stay in the Football League, Marcelo Bielsa's 100th match in charge, and the day the players would get their hands on the English Football League trophy once again. In the afternoon I headed to Elland Road for a fitting last supper at Park Fisheries with my dad and Lucca, and my mum too, who was keen to sample the fish and chips she'd heard so much about (it lived up to the hype). On the way home I was torn. Should I be going back to the ground to celebrate? Or just enjoy the match and trophy presentation with a nice bottle of Argentinian Malbec I'd bought for the occasion?

I was still split when the game started, and still split at half-time. The fact I still hadn't opened the wine showed that I really wanted to be at Elland Road, but I was finding it hard to drag myself away from a sensational exhibition of football. Ben White had scored a magnificent individual goal to kick things off, then Stuart Dallas scored a magnificent team goal to double the lead – Hernández the architect, of course. With the pressure off, Leeds had unlocked their full potential and it was a first-half performance oozing with class. When Tyler

Roberts became the first Leeds player to head a corner into the net this season (from nearly 400 corners) it was time to go. Shackleton made it 4-0 as I drove to the ground, and by the final whistle I was stood on Lowfields Road, where 5,000 fans were gathered around an open-top bus that would act as a podium for the players to show off their trophy, after the official presentation inside an empty Elland Road.

When the squad finally emerged from the East Stand I felt a surge of emotion, and the whole crowd cheered like a goal. Initially we couldn't see a thing as blue and yellow smoke engulfed the bus, but what a sight when it cleared; our heroes in white, and the beautiful, gleaming Championship trophy lofted in Liam Cooper's hands. A dream come true.

I was able to FaceTime Lewis so he could share the experience with us from Canada, though not in time to catch Berardi screaming down the microphone, 'I FEEL FUCKING GREAT!' when asked about his ACL injury. It was the opposite end of the poetic spectrum to Eric Cantona's words at the previous trophy celebration ('I don't know why, but I love you'), but it struck a similar chord. After a few minutes of singing and dancing the players waved their goodbyes. It had been short and sweet, and I will always regret not being inside Elland Road, but this was a memory I will cherish forever.

Epilogue

AFTER 16 years it had finally happened; Marcelo Bielsa had beaten the Football Gods, or the Gypsy Curse, or whatever it was that always haunted The Damned United. Leeds United were back!

It all felt so surreal, not least because no fans were there to witness the final games, but also because the end of the season had been such a whirlwind. Game after game after game, day after day after day. Heading into the last week of the season we were on tenterhooks, then suddenly it was all over and Leeds had romped it by ten points! I struggled to grasp exactly what I should be happiest about. That Leeds were no longer in the EFL? That they were a Premier League team again? That they had won a trophy? My overriding emotion was joy for Bielsa and the players, who had displayed unwavering commitment to the cause of getting Leeds United back to the Premier League and will forever be heroes at Elland Road, some of them legends.

To this day, the trophy presentation still doesn't seem real. I just can't take it in, it's too blissful! It peaked when, amid the wild celebrations, Patrick Bamford and Kalvin Phillips dragged The Great Man over to lift the trophy himself. Just as his players had done, Bielsa crouched down with the trophy before lofting it triumphantly, then humbly retreated into the background again, welling up as the squad chanted his name.

Despite running them into the ground for two years solid, the players idolised this man, and afterwards they each spoke about how much they owe to their manager, that he had improved them not only as footballers but as human beings too.

He may not like being called 'God', but Marcelo truly is godlike; in his morals, his kindness, his ability to touch people's lives, his press conference parables, and his footballing miracles. He had turned the Leeds players from water into wine. He had built a team of champions out of a squad of also-rans, without spending a penny in transfers; The Feeding of the 35,000, with five bread cakes and a double fish from Park Fisheries.

The players won the matches, Bielsa conditioned them to win, and Andrea Radrizzani's ambition and insight set the foundations for Bielsa's success. But without the passion of the fanbase Bielsa wouldn't be here; without the potential revenue of the fanbase Radrizzani wouldn't be here, and without the sustained loyalty of the fanbase the club might not be here at all. For 14 years Leeds United were the biggest joke in English football, yet through all the misery and despair the fans delivered on their promise to 'stay with you forever', and were eventually rewarded with a messiah.

The last words belong to that messiah, Marcelo Alberto Bielsa, spoken in 2015 when Leeds were at their most shambolic. El Loco's words may have been addressed to his Marseille team, but they proved a fitting prophecy to the supporters of the club he would come to save:

'Accept the injustice, swallow the poison. In the end everything finds its balance. You will have the reward you deserve.'

Championship Table 2019/20

		Pld	W	D	L	F	A	Pts
1	**LEEDS (C)**	**46**	**28**	**9**	**9**	**77**	**35**	**93**
2	West Brom (P)	46	22	17	7	77	45	83
3	Brentford	46	24	9	13	80	38	81
4	Fulham (P)	46	23	12	11	64	48	81
5	Cardiff City	46	19	16	11	68	58	73
6	Swansea City	46	18	16	12	62	53	70
7	Nottingham Forest	46	18	16	12	58	50	70
8	Millwall	46	17	17	12	57	51	68
9	Preston North End	46	18	12	16	59	54	66
10	Derby County	46	17	13	16	62	64	64
11	Blackburn Rovers	46	17	12	17	66	63	63
12	Bristol City	46	17	12	17	60	65	63
13	Queens Park Rangers	46	16	10	20	67	76	58
14	Reading	46	15	11	20	59	58	56
15	Stoke City	46	16	8	22	62	68	56
16	Sheffield Wednesday	46	15	11	20	58	66	56
17	Middlesbrough	46	13	14	19	48	61	53
18	Huddersfield Town	46	13	12	21	52	70	51
19	Luton Town	46	14	9	23	54	82	51
20	Birmingham City	46	12	14	20	54	75	50
21	Barnsley	46	12	13	21	49	69	49
22	Charlton Athletic	46	12	12	22	50	65	48
23	Wigan Athletic	46	15	14	17	57	56	47*
24	Hull City	46	12	9	25	57	87	45

* Wigan Athletic were deducted 12 points for going into administration.